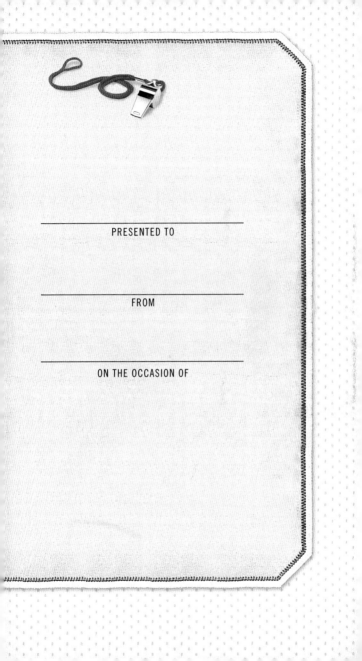

_____

PRESENTED TO

_____

FROM

_____

ON THE OCCASION OF

LIFE PROMISES *FOR* SUCCESS

JIM TRESSEL

LIFE PROMISES

FOR SUCCESS

promises from God on achieving your best

Tyndale House Publishers, Inc. · Carol Stream, Illinois

Visit Tyndale's exciting website at www.tyndale.com.

Life Promises for Success: Promises from God on Achieving Your Best

Designed by Jacqueline L. Nuñez

Library of Congress Cataloging-in-Publication Data

Tressel, Jim.
   Life promises for success : promises from God on achieving your best / Jim Tressel with Chris Fabry.
      p. cm.
   Includes bibliographical references and index.
   ISBN 978-1-4143-3728-9 (hc)
   1. Success—Religious aspects—Christianity. 2. Success—Biblical teaching. 3. God (Christianity)—Promises. I. Fabry, Chris, date. II. Title.
   BV4598.3.T74 2010
   248.4—dc22   2010014164

Printed in China

17 16 15 14 13 12 11
 8   7   6   5   4   3   2

CONTENTS

PART ONE

THE ESSENCE OF
SUCCESS

"I am only one, but I am one.
I can't do everything, but I can do something.
And what I can do, I ought to do.
And what I ought to do, by the grace of
God, I shall do."

EDWARD EVERETT HALE

LIFE PROMISES

"I know the plans I have for you," says the LORD. "They are plans for good and not for disaster, to give you a future and a hope."

JEREMIAH 29:11

Look straight ahead, and fix your eyes on what lies before you. Mark out a straight path for your feet; stay on the safe path.

PROVERBS 4:25-26

You can make many plans, but the LORD's purpose will prevail.

PROVERBS 19:21

SUCCESS IS A JOURNEY

Success is a journey that we all take, and it affects every phase of our lives. In order to thrive during that journey, we have to have a clear view of what success is, what it isn't, and what it will take to achieve it. Many people define success by how much money they make or how far up the corporate ladder they can ascend. Coaches or athletes define it in terms of championships, winning records, or great individual statistics. Championships and wins are fine goals. Goals are important, but it's important to understand that people are not *defined* by their goals and whether or not they reach them. A win or a loss does not make you or me a better or worse human being. This is where, in our society, we've so easily lost perspective on the truth about *who we are*. We have to separate who we *are* from what we *do*. Understanding the difference between purpose and goals is essential to understanding the true definition of success.

LIFE PROMISES

Those who love money will never have enough. How meaningless to think that wealth brings true happiness!

ECCLESIASTES 5:10

Commit your actions to the LORD, and your plans will succeed.

PROVERBS 16:3

Don't love money; be satisfied with what you have.

HEBREWS 13:5

How Do *You* Define Success?

John Wooden, the legendary UCLA basketball coach, is one of my heroes. In his autobiography, *They Call Me Coach,* he defines the elusive quality of success: "Success is peace of mind, which is a direct result of self-satisfaction in knowing you did your best to become the best you are capable of becoming." That's a great definition. First, it takes away any external characterization of success and puts the responsibility on the individual to define his or her own success. Coach Wooden wrote his definition in 1972, at a time when many people defined success by the kinds of cars they drove, the houses they lived in, what jobs they had, and what material possessions they owned. In other words, it was a lot like it is today. But Wooden's description of success transcends the dictionary definition. It's not the accumulation of material possessions or the gaining of a certain amount of prestige or rank. It's not moving up the ladder at work, becoming famous, or gaining political power. Success is found in "peace of mind."

LIFE PROMISES

Anyone who belongs to Christ has
become a new person. The old life
is gone; a new life has begun!

2 CORINTHIANS 5:17

God, who began the good work within
you, will continue his work until it is
finally finished on the day when Christ
Jesus returns.

PHILIPPIANS 1:6

Create in me a clean heart, O God.
Renew a loyal spirit within me.

PSALM 51:10

THE GUY IN THE GLASS

When you get what you want in your struggle for
  pelf,
And the world makes you King for a day,
Then go to the mirror and look at yourself,
And see what that guy has to say.

For it isn't your Father, or Mother, or Wife,
Who judgment upon you must pass.
The feller whose verdict counts most in your life
Is the guy staring back from the glass.

He's the feller to please, never mind all the rest,
For he's with you clear up to the end,
And you've passed your most dangerous, difficult test
If the guy in the glass is your friend.

You may be like Jack Horner and "chisel" a plum,
And think you're a wonderful guy,
But the man in the glass says you're only a bum
If you can't look him straight in the eye.

You can fool the whole world down the pathway
    of years,
And get pats on the back as you pass,
But your final reward will be heartaches and tears
If you've cheated the guy in the glass.

DALE WIMBROW

LIFE PROMISES

Blessed are those who trust in the Lord and have made the Lord their hope and confidence.

JEREMIAH 17:7

Be strong and courageous! Do not be afraid and do not panic before them. For the Lord your God will personally go ahead of you. He will neither fail you nor abandon you.

DEUTERONOMY 31:6

Be sure of this: I am with you always, even to the end of the age.

MATTHEW 28:20

What's Your *Self* Worth?

We must never let goals, adversity—or even success—define us. Those things don't hit at the heart of who we are. It's hard in today's society to keep success in its proper perspective and not base our sense of self-worth on what we do. But if we can get there, it's such a comfort. If we lose a game, a promotion, or an account, we're not losers—that's not who we are. And by the same token, if we win a game, get a promotion, or land a big deal, that doesn't make us wonderful people. We achieved our goal, and that has its place, but that success—or any failure—doesn't define us. The thing we should most enjoy about any endeavor is the road we travel together to get there.

"To be what we are, and to become what we are capable of becoming, is the only end of life."

ROBERT LOUIS STEVENSON

LIFE PROMISES

Can anything ever separate us from Christ's love? Does it mean he no longer loves us if we have trouble or calamity, or are persecuted, or hungry, or destitute, or in danger, or threatened with death? . . . No, despite all these things, overwhelming victory is ours through Christ, who loved us.

ROMANS 8:35, 37

Trust in the LORD with all your heart; do not depend on your own understanding. Seek his will in all you do, and he will show you which path to take.

PROVERBS 3:5-6

Who You Are

Many people get frustrated when they set out on a particular course and then can't reach the end. But you have to remember that success isn't necessarily doing what you thought was perfect for you when you were eighteen. As you progress through life, you may find that your purpose is a little different from what it was when you started out. Maybe you were fired from your first job, or maybe you just didn't like it. That doesn't make you a failure. Losing a job, changing your major, facing setbacks—those things don't make you a failure because they aren't about *who you are.*

"Fame usually comes to those who are thinking about something else."

OLIVER WENDELL HOLMES

LIFE PROMISES

Let's not get tired of doing what is good. At just the right time we will reap a harvest of blessing if we don't give up.

GALATIANS 6:9

Patient endurance is what you need now, so that you will continue to do God's will. Then you will receive all that he has promised.

HEBREWS 10:36

We are God's masterpiece. He has created us anew in Christ Jesus, so we can do the good things he planned for us long ago.

EPHESIANS 2:10

The True Measure of Success

Success is a journey. It is defined not by those outside of us—who give us awards or bestow honor—or even by getting that promotion or winning a championship. The true measure of success is whether we feel good about our ability to contribute to whatever team we're on. Ultimately then, to have a successful journey, we must have the faith and belief that we can and will be successful. It is vital that we be equipped and prepared for the journey and that we constantly remind ourselves of our ultimate purpose.

"We are only beaten when we cease to believe what we can be."

AUTHOR UNKNOWN

LIFE PROMISES

I can do everything through Christ, who gives me strength.

PHILIPPIANS 4:13

Dear brothers and sisters, never get tired of doing good.

2 THESSALONIANS 3:13

Whatever you do, do well.

ECCLESIASTES 9:10

THE BEST YOU CAN DO

Whether you're a business owner, you work for a corporation, you're a coach, a player, or a mother of three—no matter what circumstances are in your past and no matter what obstacles you face in the future—you *can* win in the game of life. You can succeed as long as you define success as the inner satisfaction and peace of mind that come from knowing you did the best you were capable of doing.

"The greater danger for most of us lies not in setting our aim too high and falling short; but in setting our aim too low, and achieving our mark."

MICHELANGELO

LIFE PROMISES

Let us run with endurance the race God has set before us. We do this by keeping our eyes on Jesus, the champion who initiates and perfects our faith.

HEBREWS 12:1-2

I run with purpose in every step. I am not just shadowboxing.

1 CORINTHIANS 9:26

Forgetting the past and looking forward to what lies ahead, I press on to reach the end of the race and receive the heavenly prize for which God, through Christ Jesus, is calling us.

PHILIPPIANS 3:13-14

A Grand Adventure

D r. Karl Menninger refers to hope as "an adventure, a going forward, a confident search for a rewarding life." I believe that every person needs to discover that perspective. We're all on an adventure, but some of us haven't fully embraced it. Moving forward and gaining confidence in search of true success is a lifelong endeavor. If we begin when we're young, we're able to see the changes we consciously make over the years, and we're better equipped to evaluate our progress. But even if we're not so young anymore, we can begin today to develop our purpose and set our goals for the years still to come. It's never too late to seek and find that rewarding life.

"Hope is an adventure, a going forward,
a confident search for a rewarding life."

DR. KARL MENNINGER

PART TWO

THE ELEMENTS OF
SUCCESS

"If you do the things you need to do
When you need to do them,
Someday you can do the things you want to do
When you want to do them."

AUTHOR UNKNOWN

LIFE PROMISES

Anything is possible if a person believes.

MARK 9:23

I tell you the truth, you can say to this mountain, "May you be lifted up and thrown into the sea," and it will happen.

MARK 11:23

Blessed are those who trust in the LORD and have made the LORD their hope and confidence.

JEREMIAH 17:7

THE MAN WHO THINKS HE CAN

If you think you're beaten, you are;
If you think you dare not, you don't.
If you'd like to win, but think you can't,
It's almost a cinch you won't.
If you think you'll lose, you're lost,
For out in the world we find
Success begins with a fellow's will;
It's all in the state of mind. . . .

Think big, and your deeds will grow;
Think small and you'll fall behind.
Think that you can, and you will;
It's all in the state of mind.

If you think you're outclassed, you are;
You've got to think high to rise.
You've got to be sure of yourself before
You can ever win a prize.
Life's battles don't always go
To the stronger or faster man,
But soon or late the man who wins
Is the fellow who thinks he can.
It's all in the state of mind!

WALTER D. WINTLE

LIFE PROMISES

Always be full of joy in the Lord. . . .
Don't worry about anything; instead,
pray about everything. Tell God what
you need, and thank him for all he
has done.

PHILIPPIANS 4:4, 6

Always be joyful. Never stop praying. Be
thankful in all circumstances, for this is
God's will for you who belong to Christ
Jesus.

1 THESSALONIANS 5:16-18

The LORD will work out his plans for
my life.

PSALM 138:8

TYSON GENTRY

Tyson Gentry was a third-year sophomore walk-on from Sandusky, Ohio, who was both a punter and a wide receiver for us in 2006. His dreams of being an Ohio State player were curtailed by an unfortunate injury on a routine play. He simply went up for a pass, as he'd done a thousand times before, and the next thing we knew, after a seemingly routine tackle, he was lying motionless on the field. As it turned out, he had a fracture of the C4 vertebra, about where the neck goes into the shoulders. The doctors fused the surrounding C3 and C5 vertebrae together, and today Tyson has movement in his arms and some of his upper body. His goal now is to walk again. Tyson is an amazing young man with an unbelievable attitude. He has been tenacious about his schoolwork and his physical rehabilitation, and he is a constant reminder to the guys on our team of what a real hero is. Tyson has shown us that it's not what happens to you that counts in life. It's how you handle it. I ask God to give me more of Tyson Gentry's attitude every day.

LIFE PROMISES

We are confident that he hears us whenever we ask for anything that pleases him. And since we know he hears us when we make our requests, we also know that he will give us what we ask for.

1 JOHN 5:14-15

Your Father knows exactly what you need even before you ask him!

MATTHEW 6:8

Keep on asking, and you will receive what you ask for. Keep on seeking, and you will find. Keep on knocking, and the door will be opened to you. For everyone who asks, receives. Everyone who seeks, finds. And to everyone who knocks, the door will be opened.

MATTHEW 7:7-8

ASK AND YOU SHALL RECEIVE

I asked God for strength, that I might achieve.
I was made weak, that I might learn humbly
to obey. . . .
I asked for health, that I might do greater things.
I was given infirmity, that I might do better things. . . .
I asked for riches, that I might be happy.
I was given poverty, that I might be wise. . . .
I asked for power, that I might have the praise of men.
I was given weakness, that I might feel the need
of God. . . .
I asked for all things, that I might enjoy life.
I was given life, that I might enjoy all things. . . .
I got nothing I asked for—but everything I had
hoped for;
Almost despite myself, my unspoken prayers
were answered.
I am, among men, most richly blessed!

AUTHOR UNKNOWN (OFTEN ATTRIBUTED TO AN UNKNOWN CONFEDERATE SOLDIER)

LIFE PROMISES

Do to others whatever you would like them to do to you.

MATTHEW 7:12

You have heard the law that says, "Love your neighbor" and hate your enemy. But I say, love your enemies! . . . If you love only those who love you, what reward is there for that? . . . If you are kind only to your friends, how are you different from anyone else? . . . But you are to be perfect, even as your Father in heaven is perfect.

MATTHEW 5:43-44, 46-48

Do not judge others, and you will not be judged. For you will be treated as you treat others.

MATTHEW 7:1-2

You Can't Argue with *That*

There are two things that give us a chance to have a positive impact on those who agree with us and those who don't. The first one is happiness or joy. If we consistently demonstrate that we're happy or joyful, it's very inviting to people on the outside looking in. They think, *I wonder what makes that guy tick? I wonder what makes him look at life the way he does?* Happiness tears down the walls that separate us and draws people together. Second, we can earn a hearing from other people by respecting where they are coming from and listening to their perspectives on life. If we repel people with our words and build up walls, we don't have a chance to dialogue. If we exude happiness and treat other people with respect, then perhaps the more they're around us, the more they'll want to learn about what makes us tick. To me, that's a real strength. I would want the other person to say, "Man, I don't agree with that guy, but I can't argue that he's really happy, and he always treats me well. There's something there I'd like to have."

LIFE PROMISES

Trust in the LORD with all your heart; do not depend on your own understanding. Seek his will in all you do, and he will show you which path to take.

PROVERBS 3:5-6

Faith is the confidence that what we hope for will actually happen; it gives us assurance about things we cannot see.

HEBREWS 11:1

I tell you the truth, if you had faith even as small as a mustard seed, you could say to this mountain, "Move from here to there," and it would move. Nothing would be impossible.

MATTHEW 17:20

You Gotta Believe

Faith and belief are not merely tools we use to pull ourselves up by our bootstraps and forge ahead blindly. There's a substance to our faith. There's an object for our belief. Faith is who you are. Belief is what you do with your faith. Having faith means placing your trust in something much bigger than yourself. Faith is the bedrock of a winner. It's what anchors you. It's the foundation for everything you do, and thus it's part of who you are. Belief is more personal. It's what you *do* rather than who you are. Belief is the outward expression of an inner faith. I find with groups I talk to that there's often some hesitation in people. *Can I really do this? I know I want to, but can I really do it?* It's a constant mental quiz they're taking every day. Having a deep-seated belief helps so much on the journey, and that belief is bolstered by preparation and practice. But even with all the preparation and handling what comes our way, at the end of the day we have to *believe* we can reach our goals, or it's not going to happen.

LIFE PROMISES

Be strong and courageous! Do not be afraid or discouraged. For the Lᴏʀᴅ your God is with you wherever you go.

JOSHUA 1:9

Let everything you say be good and helpful, so that your words will be an encouragement to those who hear them.

EPHESIANS 4:29

Don't worry about anything; instead, pray about everything. Tell God what you need, and thank him for all he has done. Then you will experience God's peace, which exceeds anything we can understand. His peace will guard your hearts and minds as you live in Christ Jesus.

PHILIPPIANS 4:6-7

WITHOUT A DOUBT . . .

An amazing thing happened to me just before we played the 1993 national championship game against Marshall University. Our team had gone through an incredible crucible, playing through the stress and strain and agony of that particular season. I had taken some time to be alone and had walked down a series of steps to get to the field where we would play the game. I thought about the team we were up against and all the talent they had, and it seemed like such an uphill battle for us. To be honest, I was having a few doubts about my own ability. My longtime mentor, Doc Spurgeon, saw me, and I think he kind of sensed what was going on. He came up and asked what was wrong, and I was honest with him. "Doc, I'm not sure. This is such a challenge." Without missing a beat, he looked straight at me and challenged me in his direct and eloquent way: "Wait a minute, Jim. Let me tell you something. If there were one play and I had to have one person call it, you're the only coach to whom I would say, 'Run that play.' Believe in yourself. You can do it!" I just smiled at him. There was such love in his words, and they came at just the right time for me, when I felt my resolve wavering a bit. We won that game 17–5.

LIFE PROMISES

Don't copy the behavior and customs of this world, but let God transform you into a new person by changing the way you think. Then you will learn to know God's will for you, which is good and pleasing and perfect.

ROMANS 12:2

Even children are known by the way they act, whether their conduct is pure, and whether it is right.

PROVERBS 20:11

Choose a good reputation over great riches; being held in high esteem is better than silver or gold.

PROVERBS 22:1

WHEN NO ONE ELSE IS LOOKING

Class is not a socioeconomic designation. It's not about how much money you make or don't make. It's not a way to pigeonhole people. Class is a way of life—a way of acting with confidence and style that reflects on you. It's having the freedom to do anything you want but choosing the right path. You don't want to base how you live on what other people think of you. If you do, you'll always be struggling to live up to an image, trying to figure out what will make you look good in other people's eyes. Of course, I think there's a place to ask yourself, *How do I want others to view me? If someone were to ask those people what kind of person I am, what would I want them to say?* Class is not arrogance. It doesn't put you above anyone else, and it doesn't call attention to itself; it simply treats people with respect.

"Manners are like the zero in arithmetic; they may not be much in themselves, but they are capable of adding a great deal to the value of everything else."

DAME FREYA MADELEINE STARK

LIFE PROMISES

Be an example to all believers in what
you say, in the way you live, in your
love, your faith, and your purity.

1 TIMOTHY 4:12

When you give to someone in need,
don't let your left hand know what your
right hand is doing. Give your gifts
in private, and your Father, who sees
everything, will reward you.

MATTHEW 6:3-4

Be quick to listen, slow to speak, and
slow to get angry.

JAMES 1:19

CHOOSE YOUR WORDS CAREFULLY

The words you use and the way you use them reflect the kind of person you are. Abraham Lincoln is often quoted as saying, "It is better to remain silent and be thought a fool than to speak and remove all doubt." I love that quote because it implies that keeping our mouths shut takes real discipline. I don't know how many times in my life I would have been better off just shutting my mouth and walking away rather than saying something I later regretted. If you always have to be the one in the spotlight, the one getting all the honors; if you're always building yourself up at the expense of others, at some point life is going to humble you. It's better to help others up and give of yourself. Let someone else exalt you in due time. That's the path to true honor.

"It is better to remain silent and be thought a fool than to speak and remove all doubt."

ABRAHAM LINCOLN

LIFE PROMISES

Don't use foul or abusive language. Let everything you say be good and helpful, so that your words will be an encouragement to those who hear them.

EPHESIANS 4:29

I tell you this, you must give an account on judgment day for every idle word you speak. The words you say will either acquit you or condemn you.

MATTHEW 12:36-37

In everything we do, we show that we are true ministers of God.

2 CORINTHIANS 6:4

Ten Reasons Why
I Swear

1. It pleases my mother so much.
2. It is a fine mark of manliness.
3. It proves I have self-control.
4. It indicates how clearly my mind operates.
5. It makes my conversation so pleasing to everybody.
6. It leaves no doubt in anyone's mind as to my good breeding.
7. It impresses people that I have more than an ordinary education.
8. It is an unmistakable sign of culture and refinement.
9. It makes me a very desirable personality among women, children, and respectable society.
10. It is my way of honoring God, who said, "You must not misuse the name of the Lord your God."

"Hold yourself to a higher standard than anyone expects of you. Never excuse yourself."

HENRY WARD BEECHER

LIFE PROMISES

Choose a good reputation over great
riches; being held in high esteem is
better than silver or gold.

PROVERBS 22:1

The Holy Spirit produces this kind
of fruit in our lives: love, joy, peace,
patience, kindness, goodness,
faithfulness, gentleness, and self-
control.

GALATIANS 5:22-23

Whatever you do or say, do it as a
representative of the Lord Jesus.

COLOSSIANS 3:17

Do It with Class

*C*lass is respect for others. It is a deep and genuine respect for every human being, regardless of his or her status in life.

Class is having manners. It is always saying "thank you" and "please." It is complimenting people for any and every task done well.

Class is treating every other person as you would want him or her to treat you in a similar situation.

Class never makes excuses for one's own shortcomings, but it always helps others bounce back from their mistakes.

Class never brags or boasts about one's own accomplishments, and it never tears down or diminishes the achievements of another person.

Class does not depend on money, status, success, or ancestry. The poorest man in town may radiate class in everything he does.

If you have *class*, everyone will know it, and you will have self-respect. If you are without class—good luck, because no matter what you accomplish, it will never have meaning.

LIFE PROMISES

I have learned how to be content with
whatever I have.

PHILIPPIANS 4:11

True godliness with contentment is
itself great wealth. After all, we brought
nothing with us when we came into
the world, and we can't take anything
with us when we leave it. So if we have
enough food and clothing, let us be
content.

1 TIMOTHY 6:6-8

Enjoy what you have rather than
desiring what you don't have. Just
dreaming about nice things is
meaningless—like chasing the wind.

ECCLESIASTES 6:9

THE GRASS IS *NEVER* GREENER

Voltaire once said, "Paradise is where I am." I love that quote. To me, Voltaire's statement is a lifestyle captured in five simple words. If you're in paradise where you are—not wishing you were someplace else—that's the right attitude. If you're always wishing you were someplace else, what you'll discover is that the other place has just as many problems and difficulties—maybe *more*—as the place you are right now. It's easy to think that somewhere out there is a perfect place where everyone is always happy, has a bigger house, a nicer car, and a more beautiful or handsome spouse. But that's an illusion. A mirage. If we followed Voltaire, we would see that today, right where we are, is the place God has put us—whether it's a mansion or a studio apartment. And if that's true, there can be no better place, because paradise is where we are.

*"Your life is either a celebration
or a chore. The choice is yours."*

AUTHOR UNKNOWN

LIFE PROMISES

Direct your children onto the right path, and when they are older, they will not leave it.

PROVERBS 22:6

To enjoy your work and accept your lot in life—this is indeed a gift from God. God keeps such people so busy enjoying life that they take no time to brood over the past.

ECCLESIASTES 5:19-20

There are different kinds of spiritual gifts, but the same Spirit is the source of them all. There are different kinds of service, but we serve the same Lord. God works in different ways, but it is the same God who does the work in all of us.

1 CORINTHIANS 12:4-6

Everything after That Is Gravy

I've been coaching for more than thirty years, and in that time I don't think kids have changed all that much, but parents have. Thirty years ago, parents put as their top priority their son's getting a diploma, becoming a man of good conscience, and growing as a human being. These days, with the possibility of the NFL looming, some parents—not all, but some—see a potential financial windfall. One of the things I commonly hear is, "My son needs more touches," which means that the parent wants his or her son to get the ball more. Often I respond, "Hey, you've got a great son. You are so lucky. He's a wonderful young man, and he's trying his hardest, both in the classroom and on the field. No matter what he decides to do, he's going to be successful, and he's growing in so many ways. Now I know you're not happy that he's not playing more. But you've got a great kid." If I could say anything to parents whose sons or daughters have some athletic skill, I'd say let them become good people first. Good citizens. Let them be people who care and give and want to be part of a team. Whatever happens after that is gravy.

LIFE PROMISES

For everything there is a season, a time for every activity under heaven.

ECCLESIASTES 3:1

True godliness with contentment is itself great wealth.

1 TIMOTHY 6:6

Let the peace that comes from Christ rule in your hearts. For as members of one body you are called to live in peace. And always be thankful.

COLOSSIANS 3:15

Savor the Moment

In 1991, CBS televised the Division I-AA national championship game between Youngstown State and Marshall. With about a minute to go in the game, we were up 25–17 and had a fourth-down situation with the ball deep in our own territory. So we called a time-out, and I said to our punter, "Just get the punt off." He got off a pretty good kick, leaving Marshall with a long field and not much time left on the clock. They threw one Hail Mary pass that was incomplete, and the game was over. That was my first national championship. I went out to midfield to shake hands with Jim Donnan, the Marshall coach, and a media guy ran up beside me, stuck a microphone in front of me, and said, "Do you think you'll repeat?" I kind of slowed down and looked at him. "Well, I don't know. We haven't gotten the first trophy yet, and we can't repeat until we get the first one." There's a fine line between enjoying our success and resting in our accomplishments. If we can't be happy about the success we've achieved, or be content with it, when are we ever going to relax? We'll always be chasing the next championship and never be satisfied, and that's no way to live. We must learn how to celebrate our success without being caught up in it.

LIFE PROMISES

Be careful how you live. Don't live like fools, but like those who are wise. Make the most of every opportunity.

EPHESIANS 5:15-16

Come to me, all of you who are weary and carry heavy burdens, and I will give you rest. Take my yoke upon you. Let me teach you, because I am humble and gentle at heart, and you will find rest for your souls. For my yoke is easy to bear, and the burden I give you is light.

MATTHEW 11:28-30

It is useless for you to work so hard from early morning until late at night . . . for God gives rest to his loved ones.

PSALM 127:2

Be Careful What You Wish For

Success does things to you that adversity doesn't. It adds more things to your plate. Take this book, for example. If we hadn't won as many games as we've won, no one would care about my definition of success. Success also adds a lot of people to your life—from media reps wanting answers, to friends who want tickets to the big game, to others who simply want to be seen with you. But for everything that success adds to your schedule, it takes something else away. Whether it's from your exercise time, your spiritual time, your family time, or your students' academic time, success takes away time and can distract you from your goals and plans. It's interesting that adversity has the opposite effect. When you meet with adversity, you can often find yourself alone. No one's calling to ask you to speak at a banquet. No one's interested in your opinion about success. You don't have people clamoring for your time, so you have more time to yourself. My point is that whether you have success or failure, you have a challenge ahead of you. Whether the ball bounces your way or not, everything that happens during the course of your journey is part of life, and you have to learn how to adjust.

LIFE PROMISES

It is not that we think we are qualified to do anything on our own. Our qualification comes from God.

2 CORINTHIANS 3:5

The Lord has told you what is good, and this is what he requires of you: to do what is right, to love mercy, and to walk humbly with your God.

MICAH 6:8

We will not boast about things done outside our area of authority. We will boast only about what has happened within the boundaries of the work God has given us.

2 CORINTHIANS 10:13

SUCCESS IS A LOUSY TEACHER

Microsoft founder Bill Gates has said, "Success is a lousy teacher. It makes smart people think they can't lose." I love that quote because it puts so many things in perspective. When "smart people" think they can't lose, there's an upset brewing. That's when David beats Goliath and the underdog triumphs. It's why many leading companies end up behind in the market. At one time, they were on top of things, happy with their growth and profits, but when someone suggested they needed to change in some way to remain competitive, their leaders said, in one way or another, "No, we're a winning company. We've got our market and our technology; we're not going to change anything." Then, all of a sudden, three other companies are serving the same market better, and the first company is trying to catch up. So when that statement comes from a guy like Bill Gates, who has been so successful, it makes the point even better.

LIFE PROMISES

God has not given us a spirit of fear and timidity, but of power, love, and self-discipline.

2 TIMOTHY 1:7

No discipline is enjoyable while it is happening—it's painful! But afterward there will be a peaceful harvest of right living for those who are trained in this way.

HEBREWS 12:11

Train yourself to be godly. Physical training is good, but training for godliness is much better, promising benefits in this life and in the life to come.

1 TIMOTHY 4:7-8

DISCIPLINE—IT'S A GOOD THING!

Many people think of discipline as something that's done to us if we're going the wrong way: "Stop that, or I'm going to discipline you!" Obviously, according to this definition, discipline *is* for people who do something wrong. But the truth is, the reason we're disciplined is that we're loved. Parents discipline their children to point them in a good direction. Coaches are no different. If we understand and utilize the fundamental of discipline, it will help us move *toward* our desired goals in every area of life.

"Discipline is what you do when no one else is looking! It's being considerate of the other person. Having good personal habits—you are polite, on time, and take care of business with pride."

AUTHOR UNKNOWN

LIFE PROMISES

Work with enthusiasm, as though you were working for the Lord rather than for people.

EPHESIANS 6:7

Whether you eat or drink, or whatever you do, do it all for the glory of God.

1 CORINTHIANS 10:31

You must love the Lord your God with all your heart, all your soul, and all your strength.

DEUTERONOMY 6:5

LIVING AT FULL SPEED

The word *enthusiasm* is a derivative of the Greek word *entheos,* which basically means "full of spirit, full of God." It's our hope that every team member will catch that vision and live, practice, and play in a way that's full of spirit and full of God. We've all been around the type of person that everybody considers "crazy." We say, "That guy is gung ho" or "She never stops. She's always bubbly and seems to be in a different gear from everybody else." The person who lives life at full speed is one who's full of spirit. If you are one of those people, you know that barbs can be thrown your way for being "too perky," "too energetic," or "too positive." Enthusiastic people seem to have a glow about them—perhaps because they're going a hundred miles an hour. But they're playing with their whole heart and doing it constantly.

"Flaming enthusiasm, backed by horse sense and persistence, is the quality that most frequently makes for success."

DALE CARNEGIE

LIFE PROMISES

Whatever you do, do well. For when you go to the grave, there will be no work or planning or knowledge or wisdom.

ECCLESIASTES 9:10

Never be lazy, but work hard and serve the Lord enthusiastically.

ROMANS 12:11

Let's not get tired of doing what is good. At just the right time we will reap a harvest of blessing if we don't give up. Therefore, whenever we have the opportunity, we should do good to everyone—especially to those in the family of faith.

GALATIANS 6:9-10

FIND A WAY

What I've found over the years is that enthusiasm ties in closely with gratitude and humility. People who get enthusiastic have no problem humbling themselves to become part of a team. They can easily sign on to something they believe in. That's what they do. They do everything with spirit and are usually consistently enthusiastic. There are times when you have to lie to yourself and show a little more enthusiasm than you feel. That's human nature. It's not easy to be enthusiastic about a math class, maybe, but we have to find a way to get excited. That's where great teachers can make all the difference. They have the ability to get students excited about math because *they're* excited. And when someone is full of spirit and full of God about something, it can make learning fun. We have a player that others refer to as "Full Speed." It doesn't matter whether we're walking through a play or running a drill, he's doing it full speed. Players like that can help set the tone for the whole team. Don't ever underestimate the power of an enthusiastic attitude for those around you, no matter what kind of team you're on.

LIFE PROMISES

If your gift is to encourage others, be encouraging. If it is giving, give generously. If God has given you leadership ability, take the responsibility seriously. And if you have a gift for showing kindness to others, do it gladly.

ROMANS 12:8

Encourage each other and build each other up, just as you are already doing.

1 THESSALONIANS 5:11

Let us think of ways to motivate one another to acts of love and good works.

HEBREWS 10:24

What Is Your Role?

It's hard to manufacture enthusiasm, and it's difficult to gauge, but providing enthusiasm just might be your role on any given day. You run out of that tunnel and hear the roar of the crowd. You think it's for you, and then all of a sudden you're just standing on the sideline. But if your role for that day is to encourage and provide spirit, and you do it with all your heart, it can be infectious. A player comes off the field, and maybe he's just made a bad play or his opponent has beaten him. That's your chance. That's the time to energize your teammates. We watch video taken from high above the 105,000-seat Ohio Stadium, and we can tell when something big happens. You can see the sideline come alive. If the sideline is into it, that's what it means to be full of God, full of spirit. And if your role is to be an encourager, it's just as important as being a starter that day.

"A little spark kindles a great fire."

SPANISH PROVERB

LIFE PROMISES

Let us run with endurance the race God has set before us. We do this by keeping our eyes on Jesus, the champion who initiates and perfects our faith. Because of the joy awaiting him, he endured the cross, disregarding its shame. Now he is seated in the place of honor beside God's throne. Think of all the hostility he endured from sinful people; then you won't become weary and give up.

HEBREWS 12:1-3

The Lord is the everlasting God, the Creator of all the earth. He never grows weak or weary. . . . He gives power to the weak and strength to the powerless. Even youths will become weak and tired, and young men will fall in exhaustion. But those who trust in the Lord will find new strength.

ISAIAH 40:28-31

WHAT'S MOST IMPORTANT TO YOU?

Enthusiasm really is a way to demonstrate how important your task is to you. When you're tired, how much enthusiasm you can generate is really an indication of how important something is to you. Maybe you're on a job that makes you wake up early— you work the early shift, or you teach and you have to drive to work in the cold. That's tough to be enthusiastic about. Or perhaps your spouse has cancer, and you have to be at the hospital overnight. I think of Kathy Daniels, the wife of Ohio State assistant coach Joe Daniels, who sat by her husband's bedside for ten straight days. She was exhausted, but it was so important, when Joe would wake up for two minutes, for him to see the enthusiasm, spirit, and love she showed him. And now, Joe is doing great, ready to coach again, because of great doctors and his family's spirit and enthusiasm. That's what enthusiasm is all about, and it is vitally connected to gratitude and attitude and humility. It's a powerful thing to know that someone is on your team with you, rooting and pulling for you. It can keep you going day after day.

LIFE PROMISES

Don't think you are better than you really are. Be honest in your evaluation of yourselves, measuring yourselves by the faith God has given us.

ROMANS 12:3

God has given each of you a gift from his great variety of spiritual gifts. Use them well to serve one another. . . . Then everything you do will bring glory to God through Jesus Christ. All glory and power to him forever and ever! Amen.

1 PETER 4:10-11

To those who use well what they are given, even more will be given. But from those who do nothing, even what little they have will be taken away.

LUKE 19:26

THE PURSUIT OF EXCELLENCE

If you are seeking to reach your full potential, you first need to keep in mind that achieving excellence means becoming the best *person* you can possibly be, in whatever discipline or profession you choose. You might be a stellar performer on the field—or in business or in the classroom—but if you're not living an upright life, you won't achieve your full potential. You must be willing to evaluate yourself as objectively as you can and ask yourself whether you have your priorities in order and whether there's something you could do better. Of course, we're all human, and there will be times when we won't perform our particular roles as well as we can or as well as we would like. But our *intentions* are just as important as our performance in determining how close we come to reaching our full potential. Even with the best intentions, however, we still must be willing to look at what we could do better.

"Risk more than others think is safe. Care more than others think is wise. Dream more than others think is practical. Expect more than others think is possible."

CADET MAXIM, U.S. MILITARY ACADEMY

LIFE PROMISES

I press on to reach the end of the race
and receive the heavenly prize for
which God, through Christ Jesus, is
calling us.

PHILIPPIANS 3:14

We don't look at the troubles we can see
now; rather, we fix our gaze on things
that cannot be seen. For the things
we see now will soon be gone, but the
things we cannot see will last forever.

2 CORINTHIANS 4:18

I can do everything through Christ, who
gives me strength.

PHILIPPIANS 4:13

FROM EXCELLENCE TO EMINENCE

Dr. E. Gordon Gee, president of Ohio State, is one of the most highly experienced university presidents in the nation. During his thirty-four years in higher education, he has served as president of Brown University, the University of Colorado, and West Virginia University, in addition to a previous stint at Ohio State (1990–1997). I'll never forget what he said at a press conference shortly after his return to Ohio State. He remarked that what had happened while he was gone was amazing and that OSU was clearly a place of excellence. He expressed his desire to build upon the hard work of those who had put so much into the school, and then he said, "My goal is to take Ohio State from excellence to eminence." That statement was profound. Excellence can flow from the highest position of a school or organization and wash downward over individuals and groups. It can also flow upward from seemingly insignificant people who have little rank or position but who take pride in whatever tasks they are given. Use whatever duty you've been assigned today to exemplify excellence, and see what that does for your own peace of mind as well as for the good of those around you.

LIFE PROMISES

Commit your actions to the Lord, and your plans will succeed.

PROVERBS 16:3

We are God's masterpiece. He has created us anew in Christ Jesus, so we can do the good things he planned for us long ago.

EPHESIANS 2:10

You must love the Lord your God with all your heart, all your soul, all your mind, and all your strength.

MARK 12:30

EXCELLENCE

Going *far* beyond the call of duty,
Doing *more* than others expect,
This is what excellence is all about!
And it comes from *striving*,
Maintaining the *highest* standards,
Looking after the *smallest* detail,
And going the *extra* mile.
Excellence means doing your *very* best.
In *everything!*
In *every* way.

JACK JOHNSON

*"If you can't win, make the fellow
ahead of you break the record."*

AUTHOR UNKNOWN

LIFE PROMISES

Let us hold tightly without wavering
to the hope we affirm, for God can be
trusted to keep his promise.

HEBREWS 10:23

Blessed are those who trust in the Lord
and have made the Lord their hope and
confidence. They are like trees planted
along a riverbank, with roots that reach
deep into the water. Such trees are not
bothered by the heat or worried by long
months of drought. Their leaves stay
green, and they never stop producing
fruit.

JEREMIAH 17:7-8

The Lord will work out his plans for
my life.

PSALM 138:8

TODAY FIRST

In this time of change, help me to be patient, God.
Let me not run ahead of you and your plans.
Give me courage to do only what is before me
And to keep my focus on my responsibilities.
I am tempted to daydream about the future:
However, the future is in your hands.
Thus may I be close to you in all my thoughts,
Accomplish the task before me today,
And do it with all my heart.

AUTHOR UNKNOWN

LIFE PROMISES

Let us run with endurance the race God has set before us. We do this by keeping our eyes on Jesus, the champion who initiates and perfects our faith. Because of the joy awaiting him, he endured the cross, disregarding its shame. Now he is seated in the place of honor beside God's throne.

HEBREWS 12:1-2

I don't mean to say that I have already achieved these things or that I have already reached perfection. But I press on to possess that perfection for which Christ Jesus first possessed me. No, dear brothers and sisters, I have not achieved it, but I focus on this one thing: Forgetting the past and looking forward to what lies ahead, I press on to reach the end of the race and receive the heavenly prize for which God, through Christ Jesus, is calling us.

PHILIPPIANS 3:12-14

Stay Focused!

How many times have you been sitting in church or at work and allowed yourself to drift for a moment? How about when you're talking with your children or your spouse? Is your mind racing in some other place? Because we're human, that's going to happen from time to time. It's difficult not to daydream and think about the what-ifs and if-onlys of life. It happens to people in business, in the church, and at home; no one is immune. I remember my entrance interview at the University of Akron with Gordon Larson, the athletic director at the time. The most helpful advice he gave me was to "keep your rear end and your mind in the same place." That was in 1975, and I often thought about that advice when we had success and I was rumored to be a candidate for this job or that. Fortunately, I would always remember Larson's words. You need to be where you are. And where you are right now is the best place to do as well as you can. That's such a practical exercise, and it will follow wherever you go—in the workplace, at home, and at church. When you realize you've drifted, you shake it off, and you get back on task.

LIFE PROMISES

"You must love the Lord your God with all your heart, all your soul, all your strength, and all your mind. And love your neighbor as yourself." . . . "Do this and you will live!"

LUKE 10:27-28

The Lord—who is the Spirit—makes us more and more like him as we are changed into his glorious image.

2 CORINTHIANS 3:18

If you need wisdom, ask our generous God, and he will give it to you. He will not rebuke you for asking.

JAMES 1:5

PRAYER FOR GENEROSITY

Lord, teach me to be generous.
Teach me to serve you as you deserve:
To give and not to count the cost,
To fight and not to heed the wounds,
To toil and not to seek for rest,
To labor and not to ask for reward,
Save that of knowing I am doing your will.
Amen.

AUTHOR UNKNOWN

"Nothing is worth more than this day."

JOHANN WOLFGANG VON GOETHE

LIFE PROMISES

Let the peace that comes from Christ
rule in your hearts. For as members of
one body you are called to live in peace.
And always be thankful.

COLOSSIANS 3:15

Be thankful in all circumstances, for
this is God's will for you who belong
to Christ Jesus.

1 THESSALONIANS 5:18

Since everything God created is good,
we should not reject any of it but
receive it with thanks.

1 TIMOTHY 4:4

COUNT YOUR BLESSINGS

I've studied the lives of a lot of different people, people I wanted to be like, and I've found that one common denominator is that they were sincerely grateful for their blessings. We all have things we're not excited about and things that don't go the way we want them to, but when we really step back and list our blessings, we find they far outweigh the hardships that seem for a moment to be so earthshaking. Cultivating an attitude of gratitude is like working on any other fundamental: You have to practice. We all need to keep reminding ourselves how fortunate we are.

"For today and its blessings, I owe the world an attitude of gratitude."

CLARENCE E. HODGES

LIFE PROMISES

Give thanks for everything to God the Father in the name of our Lord Jesus Christ.

EPHESIANS 5:20

Devote yourselves to prayer with an alert mind and a thankful heart.

COLOSSIANS 4:2

Always be joyful. Never stop praying. Be thankful in all circumstances, for this is God's will for you who belong to Christ Jesus.

1 THESSALONIANS 5:16-18

THE GREATEST SIN

I am a big fan of Norman Vincent Peale, and I remember an old story told about him. Someone once asked him to name the greatest sin. Now, he could have said a lot of things—there are some terrible sins—but he stopped and thought awhile before responding that the gravest sin a person could commit is the sin of ingratitude. That really stuck with me, because I don't know that we often think of ingratitude as sinful. But it really is, especially when we consider just how blessed we really are.

"It is impossible to be grateful and unhappy at the same time."

AUTHOR UNKNOWN

LIFE PROMISES

If any of you wants to be my follower,
you must turn from your selfish ways,
take up your cross daily, and follow me.
If you try to hang on to your life, you
will lose it. But if you give up your life
for my sake, you will save it.

LUKE 9:23-24

Get rid of all bitterness, rage, anger,
harsh words, and slander, as well as all
types of evil behavior. Instead, be kind
to each other, tenderhearted, forgiving
one another, just as God through Christ
has forgiven you.

EPHESIANS 4:31-32

Don't be concerned for your own good
but for the good of others.

1 CORINTHIANS 10:24

How Can I Live with Gratitude Today?

It's one thing to say, "I'm grateful and fortunate," but it's something else entirely to *live* gratefully. That's what my mom did. Every day she asked, "How can I live with gratitude today? Who can I help today?" When she was seventy-six, the doctors discovered that she had pancreatic cancer. But even as she was dying, she was grateful and served others. There's a great researcher at the James Cancer Hospital at OSU, Dr. Michael Caligiuri, who discovered a treatment for pancreatic cancer that worked in the laboratory but had never been tried on a patient. So they came to my mom and said, "Would you like to try this?" "Sure," she said. "If it works, I get to stay here with the people I love. If it doesn't, I get to go to heaven and be with the people I love. I'm just grateful for the life I've lived, and if this can advance finding the cure someday, let's go." I remember sitting with her two or three days before she died. She said, "Aw, I feel so bad. I'm not coming through for all these people. These nurses are wonderful, and I'm so appreciative of these doctors, but I can't help feeling I'm letting them down." "Mom, come on," I said, trying to encourage her. But that was the way she was. She was grateful and happy every day of her life.

LIFE PROMISES

Don't be selfish; don't try to impress others. Be humble, thinking of others as better than yourselves. Don't look out only for your own interests, but take an interest in others, too.

PHILIPPIANS 2:3-4

Everything comes from [God] and exists by his power and is intended for his glory.

ROMANS 11:36

Whatever is good and perfect comes down to us from God our Father, who created all the lights in the heavens. He never changes or casts a shifting shadow.

JAMES 1:17

GRATITUDE BEGINS AT HOME

We all have times when we've slacked off at work. That shows we're not grateful for the jobs we have. We've all neglected our relationship with God. That comes directly from a lack of gratitude. We get too busy in our own little world and let the pressures around us squeeze us into a mold that's not helpful. I read a great quote by a fourteenth-century Christian mystic named Meister Eckhart. He said, "God is at home; it is we who have gone for a walk." It hit me as soon as I read it that the reason we're out for a walk is our ingratitude. We haven't checked in at home.

"Let your heart be awakened to the transforming power of gratefulness."

SARAH BAN BREATHNACH

LIFE PROMISES

God is our refuge and strength, always
ready to help in times of trouble.

PSALM 46:1

Here on earth you will have many trials
and sorrows. But take heart, because I
have overcome the world.

JOHN 16:33

Even when I walk through the darkest
valley, I will not be afraid, for you are
close beside me. Your rod and your staff
protect and comfort me.

PSALM 23:4

DEALING WITH THE OCCASIONAL CURVEBALL

There are times in the game of life when it will seem as if things are not going very well. There are times when life departs from our familiar script and throws us something we had no idea was coming. It's tempting in those circumstances to lose faith in ourselves, in the people around us, and even in God. But if we've been planting the seeds of hope in our hearts, we'll be able to overcome the problems of life and use them not only to make ourselves stronger but also to produce something good for ourselves and those we love.

"Obstacles are those frightful things you see when you take your eyes off the goal."

HANNAH MORE

LIFE PROMISES

We know that God causes everything to work together for the good of those who love God and are called according to his purpose for them.

ROMANS 8:28

Call on me when you are in trouble, and I will rescue you, and you will give me glory.

PSALM 50:15

There is wonderful joy ahead, even though you have to endure many trials for a little while. These trials will show that your faith is genuine. It is being tested as fire tests and purifies gold— though your faith is far more precious than mere gold. So when your faith remains strong through many trials, it will bring you much praise and glory and honor on the day when Jesus Christ is revealed to the whole world.

1 PETER 1:6-7

STEP IT UP

There's an old story about a farmer whose mule fell into a dry well. The farmer heard the mule making noise and discovered the poor animal's misfortune. After assessing the situation, the farmer decided the mule wasn't worth the time and expense it would take to save it. Essentially, he lost hope in the old mule. So he called his neighbors together and asked them to help him haul dirt to bury the animal and put it out of its misery. When the first shovelfuls of dirt came down, the mule became hysterical and began to kick. But as the dirt continued to hit his back, it dawned on the creature that he should shake it off each time and step up on the growing mound of dirt beneath him. Load after load of dirt hit him square in the back, but no matter how painful it was, he shook the dirt off and stepped on it. Before long, the accumulation of dirt was such that the old mule, battered and exhausted, stepped triumphantly over the wall of the well. The dirt that had been meant to bury him had actually saved his life because of the manner in which he had responded to the situation.

LIFE PROMISES

Tune your ears to wisdom, and concentrate on understanding. Cry out for insight, and ask for understanding. Search for them as you would for silver; seek them like hidden treasures. Then you will understand what it means to fear the Lord, and you will gain knowledge of God.

PROVERBS 2:2-5

The wise are mightier than the strong, and those with knowledge grow stronger and stronger.

PROVERBS 24:5

Come and listen to my counsel. I'll share my heart with you and make you wise.

PROVERBS 1:23

PERLS'S WISDOM

I once read an interesting statement by psychiatrist Fritz Perls, who said, "Learning is discovering that something is possible." But learning is not only for the young. People of any age can learn and grow if they'll stay focused and open to what's going on around them. As we learn and understand what it takes to achieve our goals—whether it's in our spiritual lives, our family lives, academics, or athletics—there's no doubt that our hope will grow stronger.

"There is no medicine like hope,
no incentive so great, and no tonic so powerful as
expectation of something tomorrow."

ORISON SWETT MARDEN

LIFE PROMISES

Anything is possible if a person believes.

MARK 9:23

Faith is the confidence that what we hope for will actually happen; it gives us assurance about things we cannot see.

HEBREWS 11:1

All glory to God, who is able, through his mighty power at work within us, to accomplish infinitely more than we might ask or think.

EPHESIANS 3:20

BLIND FAITH

There are scientists right now at Ohio State University who believe they are on the right track to find a cure for some diseases that have killed hundreds of thousands of people. They base their belief on the evidence they see—the hard work they've done with state-of-the-art equipment. But all the best equipment in the world can't motivate a person to push forward through all the false starts, blind alleys, and other obstacles that stand between him or her and an eventual cure. Hope is an unseen ingredient in any successful endeavor.

"There can be no progress if people have no faith in tomorrow."

JOHN F. KENNEDY

LIFE PROMISES

Here on earth you will have many trials and sorrows. But take heart, because I have overcome the world.

JOHN 16:33

"I know the plans I have for you," says the Lord. "They are plans for good and not for disaster, to give you a future and a hope."

JEREMIAH 29:11

My health may fail, and my spirit may grow weak, but God remains the strength of my heart; he is mine forever.

PSALM 73:26

HALF-FULL

We live in a skeptical world. News reporters are always looking for "change," and most of the time things change for the worse rather than for the better. The constant negative drumbeat we hear about things not going well and people not doing the right things can wear us down as individuals and as a society. We tend to focus on the gloom and doom rather than on the wonderful things happening in our lives. When people are devoid of hope, they're vulnerable to the traps of naysayers who think things can't be done and look at the world through negative lenses. A person who hopes says, "Sure, there are problems; yes, there are obstacles; but the future is bright—and with hard work, we can accomplish some great things."

"Hope is putting faith to work when doubting would be easier."

AUTHOR UNKNOWN

LIFE PROMISES

Be an example to all believers in what you say, in the way you live, in your love, your faith, and your purity.

1 TIMOTHY 4:12

You are the salt of the earth. . . . You are the light of the world—like a city on a hilltop that cannot be hidden. No one lights a lamp and then puts it under a basket. Instead, a lamp is placed on a stand, where it gives light to everyone in the house. In the same way, let your good deeds shine out for all to see, so that everyone will praise your heavenly Father.

MATTHEW 5:13-16

He has given me a new song to sing, a hymn of praise to our God. Many will see what he has done and be amazed. They will put their trust in the Lord.

PSALM 40:3

Hope Springs Eternal

The quotation by Andrew Fuller—"Hope is one of the principal springs that keeps mankind in motion"—tells me that if I choose, I can be a carrier of hope. Leaders do that. They take hope with them and pass it on to others. We have to make sure that in everything we do, we exemplify hope with our lives—especially on those days when things aren't going well. Others should be able to look at our lives and see the guiding light of hope within us that turns into outward action. It's important for others to see that there's a different way to live.

"The human body experiences a powerful gravitational pull in the direction of hope."

NORMAN COUSINS

LIFE PROMISES

I will guide you along the best pathway
for your life. I will advise you and watch
over you.

PSALM 32:8

Be strong and courageous! Do not
be afraid and do not panic. . . . For
the LORD your God will personally go
ahead of you. He will neither fail you
nor abandon you.

DEUTERONOMY 31:6

I am with you always, even to the end
of the age.

MATTHEW 28:20

What the Future Holds

I don't pretend to know the future, but here are three quick things I believe are true:

1. The future for each and every one of us is going to be a mixture of good and bad. Some things we'll enjoy, and some things we won't.
2. The ratio of positives and negatives that happen to us in the future is going to be most affected by the decisions we make.
3. No matter what happens in the future, no matter what the percentage of good and bad, I really believe it's true that God will never leave us. He will always be there for us.

BISHOP THOMAS TOBIN

"We are only beaten when we cease to believe what we can be."

AUTHOR UNKNOWN

LIFE PROMISES

Humble yourselves before the Lord,
and he will lift you up in honor.

JAMES 4:10

Because of the privilege and authority
God has given me, I give each of you
this warning: Don't think you are better
than you really are. Be honest in your
evaluation of yourselves, measuring
yourselves by the faith God has
given us.

ROMANS 12:3

Pride leads to disgrace, but with
humility comes wisdom.

PROVERBS 11:2

THE POWER OF FAILURE

Former French president Charles de Gaulle once remarked, "Graveyards are full of irreplaceable men." Most of the guys who come into our program know inside that humility is important, but I'm not sure they fully understand what it really means. I'm sure that many of our failures are designed to humble us and shape us into the people we want to be. The truth is, we have to let those times do their work on us. We can fight doing that and try to keep our egos intact, but we may miss out on what we need to learn.

"Graveyards are full of irreplaceable men."

CHARLES DE GAULLE

LIFE PROMISES

Those who exalt themselves will be humbled, and those who humble themselves will be exalted.

MATTHEW 23:12

Don't be selfish; don't try to impress others. Be humble, thinking of others as better than yourselves.

PHILIPPIANS 2:3

True humility and fear of the LORD lead to riches, honor, and long life.

PROVERBS 22:4

A True MVP

In football, we can value a player for his speed, or his arm strength, or how he blasts through the line. But ultimately, it's the humble superstar that most guys seem to admire and want to emulate. Humility is a quality worth desiring. If we are really humble, after a game you won't be able to tell whether we've won or lost. Or whether people are saying nice things about us or criticizing us. I think it's important to keep the word *humility* in the front of our minds. It keeps the bad form of pride at bay. Without humility, you're left only with pride. With humility, you also have gratitude.

"If we were humble, nothing would change us—neither praise nor discouragement."

MOTHER TERESA

LIFE PROMISES

Anyone who becomes as humble as this little child is the greatest in the Kingdom of Heaven.

MATTHEW 18:4

Pride ends in humiliation, while humility brings honor.

PROVERBS 29:23

Those who are the greatest among you should take the lowest rank, and the leader should be like a servant.

LUKE 22:26

THAT SOMETHING SPECIAL

An example of a person who combines humility with gratitude is linebacker A. J. Hawk, the great Green Bay Packer and former Buckeye. He accomplished a great deal and did it in a humble way. He never asked for the spotlight. In fact, he shunned it. His playing ability drew fans, but I think his immense popularity was in large part due to the way he handled himself. He had the chance to leave college early and become a first-round draft choice in the NFL. He didn't even consider it, because I think his built-in humility told him, *I'm not worthy of that right now.* When his senior year was over, the pros were taken by the fact that A.J., who was truly worthy of being a top-ten pick in the NFL draft, was also genuinely humble and appreciative. I've often said in coaching that if your most talented players are also your hardest workers, you've got a chance for real success, because everyone looks up to those guys who produce. And if those top players also have genuine humility, you really have a chance for something special. You can just tell by the way A.J. carries himself that he is one of those guys.

LIFE PROMISES

If you listen to constructive criticism,
you will be at home among the wise.

PROVERBS 15:31

Timely advice is lovely, like golden
apples in a silver basket. To one who
listens, valid criticism is like a gold
earring or other gold jewelry.

PROVERBS 25:11-12

If you reject discipline, you only harm
yourself; but if you listen to correction,
you grow in understanding.

PROVERBS 15:32

COACH WOODEN ON CRITICISM AND PRAISE

"Fellows, you're going to receive some criticism. Some of it will be deserved and some of it will be undeserved. Either way, deserved or undeserved, you're not going to like it. You're also going to receive some praise on occasion. Some of it will be deserved and some of it will be undeserved. Either way, deserved or undeserved, you're going to like it. However, your strength as an individual depends on how you respond to both criticism and praise. If you let either one have any special effect on you, it's going to hurt us. Whether it is criticism or praise, deserved or undeserved, makes no difference. If we let it affect us, it hurts us. . . . You have little control over what criticism or praise outsiders send your way. Take it all with a grain of salt. Let your opponent get all caught up in other people's opinions. But don't you do it."

"Champions believe in themselves even if no one else does."

AUTHOR UNKNOWN

LIFE PROMISES

Those who are last now will be first
then, and those who are first will
be last.

MATTHEW 20:16

Those who exalt themselves will be
humbled, and those who humble
themselves will be exalted.

MATTHEW 23:12

Do not twist justice in legal matters by
favoring the poor or being partial to the
rich and powerful. Always judge people
fairly.

LEVITICUS 19:15

HER NAME WAS DOROTHY

During my second month of college, our professor gave us a pop quiz. I was a conscientious student and had breezed through the questions, until I read the last one: "What is the first name of the woman who cleans the school?" Surely, this was some kind of joke. I had seen the cleaning woman several times. She was tall, dark-haired, and in her fifties, but how would I know her name? I handed in my paper, leaving the last question blank. Just before class ended, one student asked if the last question would count toward our quiz grade. "Absolutely," said the professor. "In your careers, you will meet many people. All are significant. They deserve your attention and care, even if all you do is smile and say, 'Hello.'"

I've never forgotten that lesson. I also learned her name was Dorothy.

"The true measure of a man is how he treats someone who can do him absolutely no good."

ANN LANDERS

LIFE PROMISES

Commit everything you do to the LORD.
Trust him, and he will help you.

PSALM 37:5

If your gift is to encourage others,
be encouraging. If it is giving,
give generously. If God has given
you leadership ability, take the
responsibility seriously. And if you
have a gift for showing kindness to
others, do it gladly.

ROMANS 12:8

The LORD will withhold no good thing
from those who do what is right.

PSALM 84:11

ONE HUNDRED PERCENT

Whatever your role, and no matter how small you think that role is, the team has to be able to count on you. You have to do your job and do it well, with all your heart. There is a story—I don't know if it's true—of a pilot who ejected from the airplane, pulled his rip cord, and made it safely to the ground. He had never thought about the importance of having a working parachute, so when he got on the ground and was folding up his parachute, he looked at the name on the inspection tag. It was his own grandmother's. You'd better be able to count on the airplane mechanic or the person who inspected your parachute or the guy who installed the brakes on your car. You'd better hope that person has integrity on the job and isn't just going through the motions. That's what responsibility is.

"It takes less time to do the right thing than to explain why you did it wrong."

HENRY WADSWORTH LONGFELLOW

LIFE PROMISES

I know, my God, that you examine our hearts and rejoice when you find integrity there.

1 CHRONICLES 29:17

If you keep yourself pure, you will be a special utensil for honorable use. Your life will be clean, and you will be ready for the Master to use you for every good work.

2 TIMOTHY 2:21

People with integrity walk safely, but those who follow crooked paths will slip and fall.

PROVERBS 10:9

GANDHI

Toward the end of Mohandas Gandhi's extraordinary life, he listed the seven deadly sins he had encountered along the way:

Wealth without work
Pleasure without conscience
Knowledge without character
Business without morality
Science without humanity
Worship without sacrifice
Politics without principles

"I arise in the morning torn between a desire to improve the world and a desire to enjoy the world."

E. B. WHITE

LIFE PROMISES

God showed his great love for us by sending Christ to die for us while we were still sinners.

ROMANS 5:8

This is my commandment: Love each other in the same way I have loved you.

JOHN 15:12

Above all, clothe yourselves with love, which binds us all together in perfect harmony.

COLOSSIANS 3:14

Love your neighbor as yourself.

MATTHEW 22:39

Nobody Cares What You Know till They Know That You Care

Of the people you have worked for, how many can you honestly say cared about you as a person and not just as another cog in the corporate machine? My guess is that if you've had a boss or a manager who was truly interested in you and your goals in the work environment and cared about you personally, you will never forget his or her kindness. The wonderful thing about showing genuine concern for other people is that the giver gains as much as the receiver, if not more. There is a by-product of love for both giver and receiver that can't be quantified on a spreadsheet. Loving others is not easy. You have to make time for it in your busy schedule. It has to be an intentional part of your plan, one that you put in writing. And love's schedule is not always convenient. It's easy to say you want to show love, but it's something else to truly commit yourself to doing it.

"When you help someone up a hill, you get that much closer to the top yourself."

AUTHOR UNKNOWN

LIFE PROMISES

Love each other. Just as I have loved you, you should love each other. Your love for one another will prove to the world that you are my disciples.

JOHN 13:34-35

We love each other because he loved us first.

1 JOHN 4:19

Be kind to each other, tenderhearted, forgiving one another, just as God through Christ has forgiven you.

EPHESIANS 4:32

A Simple Gesture

Mark was walking home from school one day when the boy ahead of him tripped and dropped all the books he was carrying, along with two sweaters, a baseball bat, a glove, and a small tape recorder. Mark knelt down and helped the boy pick up. . . . Since they were going the same way, he helped carry part of the burden. As they walked, Mark discovered the boy's name was Bill; that he loved video games, baseball, and history; that he was having a lot of trouble with his other subjects; and that he had just broken up with his girlfriend. They continued to see each other around school . . . and had brief contact over the years. . . . Three weeks before graduation, Bill asked Mark if they could talk. . . . "Do you ever wonder why I was carrying so many things home that day?" asked Bill. "You see, I cleaned out my locker because I didn't want to leave a mess for anyone else. . . . I was going home to commit suicide. But after we spent some time together talking and laughing, I realized that if I had killed myself, I would've missed that time and so many others that might follow. So you see, Mark, when you picked up my books that day, you did a lot more. You saved my life."

JOHN W. SCHLATTER

LIFE PROMISES

Love is patient and kind. Love is not
jealous or boastful or proud or rude.
It does not demand its own way. It is
not irritable, and it keeps no record
of being wronged. It does not rejoice
about injustice but rejoices whenever
the truth wins out. Love never gives up,
never loses faith, is always hopeful, and
endures through every circumstance.

1 CORINTHIANS 13:4-7

God loved the world so much that
he gave his one and only Son, so that
everyone who believes in him will not
perish but have eternal life.

JOHN 3:16

Three things will last forever—faith,
hope, and love—and the greatest of
these is love.

1 CORINTHIANS 13:13

WHERE THERE'S A WILL . . .

Commitment is the key to every relationship. Whatever team you're on, whether it's a marriage, a family, a work team, or a sports team, in order to achieve whatever goals you've set, you must be bound together by a love that exhibits itself in extreme commitment and the laying down of one's life for the common good. The failure to commit ourselves is evident in so many aspects of our society. People want to be "cool" rather than committed. They want to be esteemed and lifted up. But you can't focus on being cool if you want to be a champion. You have to be willing to cry. You have to be willing to love. You have to be willing to commit. When I became head coach at Ohio State, my dear friend and mentor Doc Spurgeon told me about a friend of his who had been watching Ohio State's games on television. His friend's assessment of our performance was that we had played only one half of one game that season in a halfway decent fashion. "You want me to tell you what the problem is with Ohio State?" the man asked Doc. "They think you win tough games with talent. You don't win tough games with talent. You win tough games with toughness. And the way you get tough is through love."

LIFE PROMISES

There is no greater love than to lay down one's life for one's friends.

JOHN 15:13

Love each other with genuine affection, and take delight in honoring each other.

ROMANS 12:10

Live a life filled with love, following the example of Christ. He loved us and offered himself as a sacrifice for us.

EPHESIANS 5:2

Your love for one another will prove to the world that you are my disciples.

JOHN 13:35

ALL FOR LOVE

When Youngstown State played Eastern Kentucky, a defensive lapse near the end of the game put us in a desperate situation. With about two minutes to go, Eastern Kentucky completed a screen pass and scored a touchdown that put them ahead. Our linebacker, Reggie Lee, was devastated because he blamed himself for the touchdown. He was on the sideline with a world of hurt on his back. He knew he had let his teammates down, and that left him on the brink of despair. We got the ball back, and on the ensuing possession, one of our wide receivers, Darnell Bracy, made an incredible catch—it was an unbelievable play—and ran the ball in for a touchdown. We won the game.

On that one play, Reggie Lee learned what love really means. Darnell Bracy had picked up his teammate with that touchdown score. Reggie had gone from despair to hope in one play. He had seen the effects of love firsthand. A skeptic might say that the receiver wasn't catching that ball out of love; he just wanted to win the game. You're right to say that Darnell wanted to win, but there was no "just" about it. Love has a way of making unexpected things happen. Love can transform a team of players with less-than-stellar talent into a tightly knit group that can perform above their level of ability.

LIFE PROMISES

Give freely and become more wealthy;
be stingy and lose everything. The
generous will prosper; those who
refresh others will themselves be
refreshed.

PROVERBS 11:24-25

Feed the hungry, and help those in
trouble. Then your light will shine out
from the darkness, and the darkness
around you will be as bright as noon.

ISAIAH 58:10

It is more blessed to give than to
receive.

ACTS 20:35

THE PLEASURE PRINCIPLE

My friend and mentor Doc Spurgeon says that 99 percent of the people who say they love someone or something say it because that person or thing gives them pleasure. But the true measure of our love for someone or something is how much we give back to the object of our love. What are we contributing to our families, our churches, our jobs? Are we giving back to God? Everyone who wins says, "Thank you, God. I love you." You see it after games or when people are being interviewed about winning the lottery. What they're saying is, "This gives me pleasure." Or maybe they're thinking, *We won the championship, so now I'll get a new contract,* or *I scored a touchdown. Thank you, God. Maybe now I'll get drafted in the first round.* True success, however, comes from working in the opposite direction. True success is achieved when our main concern is the good of others and the building up of the team.

"Love cures all people—both the ones who give it and the ones who receive it."

DR. KARL MENNINGER

LIFE PROMISES

If any of you wants to be my follower, you must turn from your selfish ways, take up your cross daily, and follow me. If you try to hang on to your life, you will lose it. But if you give up your life for my sake, you will save it.

LUKE 9:23-24

Everyone who has given up houses or brothers or sisters or father or mother or children or property, for my sake, will receive a hundred times as much in return and will inherit eternal life.

MATTHEW 19:29

There is no greater love than to lay down one's life for one's friends.

JOHN 15:13

THE HALLMARK
OF CHAMPIONS

All coaches talk about the importance of everyone placing the team before the individual, but to stop at this point is to miss the most critical part of the message. These same coaches almost always talk of sacrifice; teamwork is a privilege. If the giver looks at the giving as a sacrifice, the giving will never be total and absolute. It is only when the giver looks at the giving as a rare privilege to be entered into with enthusiasm and joyousness that the giving is total and absolute and will carry the greatest impact. We speak here of the joy that will come to the one who loses his life to gain it. When the giver gives with all his heart and soul, he begins to understand the nature of love because *love is giving.* The greater the giving, the greater the love. It is the total and absolute giving of one's self with enthusiasm and joy that separates the exceptional from the excellent. This giving becomes the highest expression of love. If we hope to reach the top of the mountain, all of us must happily present the gift of our love through the absolute giving of ourselves to our comrades on the journey. *This love is the hallmark of champions!*

LIFE PROMISES

We can rejoice, too, when we run into problems and trials, for we know that they help us develop endurance. And endurance develops strength of character, and character strengthens our confident hope of salvation.

ROMANS 5:3-4

Our present troubles are small and won't last very long. Yet they produce for us a glory that vastly outweighs them and will last forever!

2 CORINTHIANS 4:17

These trials will show that your faith is genuine. It is being tested as fire tests and purifies gold. . . . So when your faith remains strong through many trials, it will bring you much praise and glory and honor on the day when Jesus Christ is revealed to the whole world.

1 PETER 1:7

FACING ADVERSITY

Adversity comes to us all—it's only a matter of when. The real question is not *whether* we'll face adversity but how we will respond to it when it comes. If our attitude is one that embraces learning and growing, we'll treat adversity as a stepping-stone to the success we desire, rather than see it as an insurmountable obstacle. But if we have a negative attitude and become defensive at the first hint of criticism or begin to blame others for our mistakes, we'll miss the opportunity to develop into the types of people we want to be.

"In the middle of difficulty lies opportunity."

ALBERT EINSTEIN

LIFE PROMISES

When troubles come your way, consider it an opportunity for great joy. For you know that when your faith is tested, your endurance has a chance to grow. So let it grow, for when your endurance is fully developed, you will be perfect and complete, needing nothing.

JAMES 1:2-4

I have not achieved it, but I focus on this one thing: Forgetting the past and looking forward to what lies ahead, I press on to reach the end of the race and receive the heavenly prize for which God, through Christ Jesus, is calling us.

PHILIPPIANS 3:13-14

TO LOSE IS TO WIN

I have learned more from losing than I've ever learned from winning. As a head coach, an assistant coach, and a player, the defeats taught me more than the victories did. When you compare the value of the two, it's not even close. The takeaway value of loss is so much greater. The same has been true for every team I've ever coached. We have learned more over the years from losing than from winning. And the knowledge we have gained from those losses has helped us win more games. That may sound strange, but every coach and player reading this knows exactly what I'm talking about. On the journey of success, we begin with plans, goals, and dreams. Once we have those figured out, we get to work. In the process, we invariably face hardship and struggle, as well as triumph and achievement. But whether we face success or adversity, we can learn how to not just "handle" it but to *take advantage* of it. If we want to succeed in life, we must learn how to make the most of both victory and defeat—because we're certain to encounter both along the way.

LIFE PROMISES

It is not that we think we are qualified
to do anything on our own. Our
qualification comes from God.

2 CORINTHIANS 3:5

Serve each other in humility, for "God
opposes the proud but favors the
humble."

1 PETER 5:5

We give great honor to those who
endure under suffering.

JAMES 5:11

WHEN THE GOING GETS TOUGH . . .

In my opinion, it's a lot more difficult to handle success than adversity. That's because of a natural human tendency to rest on our laurels when we've done well. If we get punched in the nose, we have an instinctual desire to fight back. If we're knocked down, we get up ready to respond in kind. And if we don't do well during a day's work, we steel ourselves and say, "I'm not going to let that happen tomorrow." When the going gets tough, our internal survival instinct compels us to press on and make things better. But I'm not sure that instinct works the same way when we've been successful. When we get accolades and people tell us how great we are, instead of responding with humility and getting back to work, our tendency is to agree with what we're hearing. We say to ourselves, *Well, we've certainly arrived. We have this thing figured out now. We're something, all right.* When we get puffed up and believe our own press, we're ripe for a fall. There will be days when everything goes right and days when it all falls apart. We'll have stretches where really good things happen, and other stretches when we can't even remember the good things. We have to be able to make the most of both the positives and the negatives.

LIFE PROMISES

I can do everything through Christ, who gives me strength.

PHILIPPIANS 4:13

As soon as I pray, you answer me; you encourage me by giving me strength.

PSALM 138:3

Don't be afraid, for I am with you. Don't be discouraged, for I am your God. I will strengthen you and help you. I will hold you up with my victorious right hand.

ISAIAH 41:10

With God's help we will do mighty things.

PSALM 60:12

IT COULDN'T BE DONE

Somebody said that it couldn't be done,
But he, with a chuckle, replied
That "maybe it couldn't," but he would be one
Who wouldn't say so till he'd tried.
So he buckled right in, with a trace of a grin
On his face. If he worried, he hid it.
He started to sing as he tackled the thing
That couldn't be done, and he did it. . . .

There are thousands to tell you it cannot be done;
There are thousands to prophesy failure;
There are thousands to point out to you, one by one,
The dangers that wait to assail you;
But just buckle right in, with a bit of a grin,
Then take off your coat and go to it;
Just start in to sing as you tackle the thing
That "cannot be done," and you'll do it!

EDGAR A. GUEST

LIFE PROMISES

I have refined you, but not as silver is refined. Rather, I have refined you in the furnace of suffering.

ISAIAH 48:10

God blesses those who patiently endure testing and temptation. Afterward they will receive the crown of life that God has promised to those who love him.

JAMES 1:12

The Lord is faithful; he will strengthen you.

2 THESSALONIANS 3:3

Woohitike (Bravery)

Woohitike (wo-oh-hee-tee-keh), or bravery, is one of the central virtues or values of the Lakota Sioux. They believe that we all have it in us to be brave, that each of us can defend the camp when necessary. Life will give us the opportunity, issuing the invitation to the contest, and as time goes on, we will be shaped and strengthened by our challenges. Whether we can win each time or not, we will be tempered by adversity. The ancient Lakota hunter warriors handcrafted their own bows from seasoned ash wood. There were two ways to acquire the proper wood. The conventional way was to find a young ash tree, harvest it, and let it dry for at least five years. But the hunter warriors were always on the lookout for a mature ash tree that had been struck by lightning. Such a tree had been dried and cured in an instant by the awesome power of lightning, and any bows made from it would be much stronger. Such trees were rare, but they were preferred because they had suffered the ultimate adversity, and ultimate adversity produces ultimate strength.

LIFE PROMISES

We are hunted down, but never
abandoned by God. We get knocked
down, but we are not destroyed.

2 CORINTHIANS 4:9

Let's not get tired of doing what is good.
At just the right time we will reap a
harvest of blessing if we don't give up.

GALATIANS 6:9

When troubles come your way, consider
it an opportunity for great joy. For you
know that when your faith is tested,
your endurance has a chance to grow.
So let it grow, for when your endurance
is fully developed, you will be perfect
and complete, needing nothing.

JAMES 1:2-4

WHEN THE PRESSURE'S ON

How do you act when the pressure's on
When the chance for victory is almost gone,
When Fortune's star has refused to shine,
When the ball is on your five-yard line?
How do you act when the going's rough,
Does your spirit lag when breaks are tough?
Or, is there in you a flame that glows
Brighter as fiercer the battle grows?
How hard, how long will you fight the foe?
That's what the world would like to know!
Cowards can fight when they're out ahead.
The uphill grind shows a thoroughbred!
You wish for success? Then tell me, son,
How do you act when the pressure's on?

AUTHOR UNKNOWN

"There is no education like adversity."

BENJAMIN DISRAELI

LIFE PROMISES

Great is his faithfulness; his mercies begin afresh each morning.

LAMENTATIONS 3:23

We can rejoice, too, when we run into problems and trials, for we know that they help us develop endurance.

ROMANS 5:3

With God's help we will do mighty things.

PSALM 60:12

UNSTOPPABLE

When we possess the hope and belief that ultimately we're going to be successful in our journeys, there's not much of what comes our way on a daily basis that we can't handle. When we see negative events as stepping-stones and have hope that our problems can actually propel us toward our goals rather than hinder us, then we are, of all people, truly blessed.

"Face adversity promptly and without flinching, and you will reduce its impact. Never run from anything and never quit."

WINSTON CHURCHILL

LIFE PROMISES

The godly may trip seven times, but they will get up again. But one disaster is enough to overthrow the wicked.

PROVERBS 24:16

Be truly glad. There is wonderful joy ahead, even though you have to endure many trials for a little while.

1 PETER 1:6

Commit everything you do to the Lord. Trust him, and he will help you.

PSALM 37:5

PAIN IS ONLY TEMPORARY

Life is a series of ups and downs, peaks and valleys, wins and losses. When the bad times come, and they inevitably will, the seeds we've sown in our lives— what we believe in and hang on to and what we know is true and right—will help us maintain the hope that whatever stands before us is not permanent but only a temporary obstacle.

"With champions, success is never unexpected; it's a natural result that comes from continuous, unselfish, unrelenting determination to win, never letting down, never letting outside influences into the game."

HARVEY MACKAY

LIFE PROMISES

The temptations in your life are no different from what others experience. And God is faithful. He will not allow the temptation to be more than you can stand. When you are tempted, he will show you a way out so that you can endure.

1 CORINTHIANS 10:13

In his kindness God called you to share in his eternal glory by means of Christ Jesus. So after you have suffered a little while, he will restore, support, and strengthen you, and he will place you on a firm foundation.

1 PETER 5:10

If God is for us, who can ever be against us?

ROMANS 8:31

NEVER GIVE UP!

In every phase of life, you're going to face opposition. There will be times when your diet is going great, your exercise program is fantastic, and you feel healthy and look great. Every morning, you get up on time, and you've hit a routine that works for you. Then something happens to derail your train. The reasons may be legitimate. Your mother gets sick, and you're driving back and forth three hours each way, and you have no time to exercise. And because you're constantly on the road, your diet suffers because you're eating fast food just to survive. That's a reality for many people. In every phase of life, there will be good pressures and bad pressures on your life. You have to learn how to handle those and respond well. If you're aware of the pressures, if you're *present* and are able to *identify* what you did wrong, you can also figure out how to *improve* the next time, and then *implement* what you've learned. If you follow this three-step process—identify, improve, and implement—you'll not only cope with adversity, but you'll also move forward stronger and with more passion toward your goals.

LIFE PROMISES

When troubles come your way, consider
it an opportunity for great joy. For you
know that when your faith is tested,
your endurance has a chance to grow.
So let it grow, for when your endurance
is fully developed, you will be perfect
and complete, needing nothing.

JAMES 1:2-4

The godly may trip seven times, but
they will get up again. But one disaster
is enough to overthrow the wicked.

PROVERBS 24:16

The Lord directs the steps of the godly.
He delights in every detail of their lives.
Though they stumble, they will never
fall, for the Lord holds them by the
hand.

PSALM 37:23-24

If at First . . .

Persistence is the key to the success of any team, business, endeavor, or person. It takes the focus away from the performance and puts it on the process. Okay, that play, that business plan, that decision you made didn't work. You didn't sell as many books or burgers or whatever you were trying to sell. But in those situations, *you* are not a failure. The bad things that happened didn't make you a failure. It simply means that the plan you had in place didn't work, so you have to get better. If you don't improve, you may no longer be employed—but that doesn't make you a failure either. Everything that happens—good and bad—should motivate you to be *persistent*. When things don't go your way, back up and start over. Learn what you can do to improve, and get back in the game.

"Many of life's failures are people who did not realize how close they were to success when they gave up."

THOMAS EDISON

LIFE PROMISES

Patient endurance is what you need now, so that you will continue to do God's will. Then you will receive all that he has promised.

HEBREWS 10:36

Keep on asking, and you will receive what you ask for. Keep on seeking, and you will find. Keep on knocking, and the door will be opened to you. For everyone who asks, receives. Everyone who seeks, finds. And to everyone who knocks, the door will be opened.

MATTHEW 7:7-8

Let us run with endurance the race God has set before us. We do this by keeping our eyes on Jesus, the champion who initiates and perfects our faith.

HEBREWS 12:1-2

SLOW AND STEADY

I grew up observing the quality of persistence in my father. He was methodical in his work, slowly building from one year to the next, and stayed at one place, Baldwin-Wallace, for twenty-three years. He'd have one year that was good and then two that were very average. In those days, you could build a program slowly, over time. I'm not sure that if he were coaching today, they'd let him work that way. I was at Youngstown State for fifteen years, which at that level is pretty unusual. I attribute that longevity to persistence. Today, people are on the move a whole lot more. The average pastor changes churches every few years. People who work in media want to move up to a bigger market so they can make more money. Seldom do you find a person who stays in one place for very long, and I suppose there are a million reasons for that. In a world that values results over everything else, we need to be persistent to pursue and achieve our goals. We're no longer just competing regionally or nationally—we're competing with the whole world in a growing global economy. We can have our legs taken out from under us pretty quickly these days. So we have to adapt and learn and *persist* if we want our work to move forward.

LIFE PROMISES

We are pressed on every side by troubles, but we are not crushed. We are perplexed, but not driven to despair. . . . We get knocked down, but we are not destroyed.

2 CORINTHIANS 4:8-9

I have fought the good fight, I have finished the race, and I have remained faithful.

2 TIMOTHY 4:7

We know that God causes everything to work together for the good of those who love God and are called according to his purpose for them.

ROMANS 8:28

ANYTIME YOU FEEL LIKE QUITTING . . .

Whenever the going gets tough, encourage yourself with the following example of persistence:

He failed in business in '32.

He ran for the state legislature in '32 and lost.

He tried business again in '33 and failed.

His sweetheart died in '35.

He had a nervous breakdown in '36.

He ran for state elector in '40 after he regained his health.

He was defeated for Congress in '43, defeated again for Congress in '48, defeated when he ran for the Senate in '55, and defeated for vice president of the United States in '56.

He ran for the Senate again in '58 and lost.

Even after all his failures, this man refused to quit. He kept trying, until in 1860 he was elected president of the United States. By now you know that this man was Abraham Lincoln.

"The greater the obstacle, the more glory in overcoming it."

MOLIÈRE

LIFE PROMISES

All glory to God, who is able, through his mighty power at work within us, to accomplish infinitely more than we might ask or think.

EPHESIANS 3:20

Be strong and courageous, and do the work. Don't be afraid or discouraged, for the LORD God, my God, is with you. He will not fail you or forsake you.

1 CHRONICLES 28:20

Whatever you do or say, do it as a representative of the Lord Jesus, giving thanks through him to God the Father.

COLOSSIANS 3:17

HOW DO YOU SEE IT?

Two stone cutters were asked what they were doing. The first one said, "I'm cutting this stone into blocks."

The second one replied, "I'm on a team that's building a cathedral."

"The quality of a person's life is in direct proportion to their commitment to excellence, regardless of their chosen field of endeavor."

VINCE LOMBARDI

LIFE PROMISES

Everything we have has come from you, and we give you only what you first gave us!

1 CHRONICLES 29:14

When you give to someone in need, don't let your left hand know what your right hand is doing. Give your gifts in private, and your Father, who sees everything, will reward you.

MATTHEW 6:3-4

God loved the world so much that he gave his one and only Son, so that everyone who believes in him will not perish but have eternal life.

JOHN 3:16

GIVING WHEN IT COUNTS

Many years ago, when I worked as a volunteer at Stanford Hospital, I got to know a little girl named Liza who was suffering from a rare and serious disease. Her only chance of recovery appeared to be a blood transfusion from her five-year-old brother, who had miraculously survived the same disease and had developed the antibodies needed to combat the illness. The doctor explained the situation to Liza's little brother and asked him if he would be willing to give his blood to his sister. I saw him hesitate for only a moment before he took a deep breath and said, "Yes, I'll do it if it will save Liza." As the transfusion progressed, he lay in his bed next to his sister and smiled, as we all did, seeing the color returning to her cheeks. Then his face grew pale, and his smile faded. He looked up at the doctor and asked with a trembling voice, "Will I start to die right away?" Being young, the boy had misunderstood the doctor; he thought he was going to have to give his sister *all* of his blood.

DAN MILLMAN

LIFE PROMISES

Don't be concerned for your own good but for the good of others.

1 CORINTHIANS 10:24

Don't be selfish; don't try to impress others. Be humble, thinking of others as better than yourselves.

PHILIPPIANS 2:3

If you try to hang on to your life, you will lose it. But if you give up your life for my sake, you will save it.

MATTHEW 16:25

It's Better to Give . . .

Dr. Pat "Doc" Spurgeon, my good friend and mentor, has told me many times that every great team has two vital ingredients: love for one another and discipline. The great thing about that combination is that you don't have to worry about discipline if you have love. If the players really care about each other—not just for show but with a genuine love that is pure and giving —they will play their roles properly. Chris Creighton, the head football coach at Drake University in Iowa, has always been one of my favorites. When he was still a young coach at Wabash College, he came up with the idea of asking coaches who had won a national championship what the most important characteristic of their championship teams was. When he asked me that question, I thought about it a long time, and the word that popped into my mind was *unselfishness*. Every championship team I've been with has been unselfish. Guys weren't worried about their rushing stats, or how many tackles, interceptions, or catches they'd made, or how many points they'd scored. They were concerned primarily about the team. And because we had teams full of unselfish people, we were able to accomplish extraordinary things together.

LIFE PROMISES

The human body has many parts, but the many parts make up one whole body. So it is with the body of Christ.

1 CORINTHIANS 12:12

We are many parts of one body, and we all belong to each other. In his grace, God has given us different gifts for doing certain things well.

ROMANS 12:5-6

If one part suffers, all the parts suffer with it, and if one part is honored, all the parts are glad.

1 CORINTHIANS 12:26

PART OF THE WHOLE

I believe that unselfishness is the number one quality exhibited by all great teams. How does unselfishness work itself out in your business, your family, or your church? Spiritually speaking, people who are part of a church are part of a body of believers. How many times have you heard of someone making bad decisions that reflected poorly on his or her church or other Christians? That person has failed to see how interconnected he or she is to the whole body. If you work for a business, are you more concerned about yourself or about the entire group? Do you care about the committee, the event being planned, your department, your individual goals, and the position you're striving for, or can you look at the entire company in an unselfish way? If we really desire success, if we want the inner satisfaction and peace that come from knowing we did all we could for the group, then we'll begin looking at the teams we're part of in a healthy way.

"He climbs highest who helps another up."

ZIG ZIGLAR

LIFE PROMISES

Give, and you will receive. Your gift will return to you in full—pressed down, shaken together to make room for more, running over, and poured into your lap. The amount you give will determine the amount you get back.

LUKE 6:38

Give generously to the poor, not grudgingly, for the Lord your God will bless you in everything you do.

DEUTERONOMY 15:10

Don't store up treasures here on earth, where moths eat them and rust destroys them, and where thieves break in and steal. Store your treasures in heaven, where moths and rust cannot destroy, and thieves do not break in and steal. Wherever your treasure is, there the desires of your heart will also be.

MATTHEW 6:19-21

MONEY ISN'T EVERYTHING

If your career goal is to make a million dollars, that's fine. The question is, what are you going to do with that money when you reach your goal? Are you planning to benefit all of society, or are you thinking only about making money for yourself? As human beings, we were not made only to achieve *things*. From the moment we're born to the moment we die, life is about relationships. True winners have compassion for others and find their greatest success not in their own accomplishments, but in helping those around them achieve.

"Concern for man and his fate must always form the chief interest of all technical endeavors. Never forget this in the midst of your diagrams and equations."

ALBERT EINSTEIN

LIFE PROMISES

Get rid of all bitterness, rage, anger.
. . . Instead, be kind to each other,
tenderhearted, forgiving one another,
just as God through Christ has forgiven
you.

EPHESIANS 4:31-32

Pay careful attention to your own work,
for then you will get the satisfaction of
a job well done, and you won't need to
compare yourself to anyone else.

GALATIANS 6:4

The Lord rewarded me for doing right.
He has seen my innocence. To the
faithful you show yourself faithful; to
those with integrity you show integrity.

PSALM 18:24-25

COMPETITIVE *DISADVANTAGE*

I t's human nature to be competitive and territorial. In a company, people can become so focused on their own success that they celebrate when someone in another department fails. Competition for goals and dreams inside a company isn't necessarily a negative thing; it can motivate employees to work harder. But when they get so focused on themselves and fail to work for the good of the team, everyone loses. Even minor victories will be hollow.

"When your organization operates like a strong family, you can't be knocked out by one punch."

MIKE KRZYZEWSKI

LIFE PROMISES

Make allowances for each other's faults,
and forgive anyone who offends you.
Remember, the Lord forgave you, so
you must forgive others.

COLOSSIANS 3:13

I will give you a new heart, and I will
put a new spirit in you. I will take out
your stony, stubborn heart and give
you a tender, responsive heart.

EZEKIEL 36:26

Don't copy the behavior and customs
of this world, but let God transform you
into a new person by changing the way
you think. Then you will learn to know
God's will for you, which is good and
pleasing and perfect.

ROMANS 12:2

WE'RE ONLY HUMAN

We're all human, and we all want to feel good about ourselves. That's why, when someone else doesn't do well, in a perverse way it can make us feel better about ourselves. That's an immature way of thinking, but it's a reality. I believe that God knows our frailty and that he wants us to recognize that foolish, selfish thinking and discard it. We have to repent of it. We have to work on our team skills every day because we're never entirely squared away in anything we do; growth is always a process, no matter who we are. People who say they don't have petty thoughts occasionally are either far better than anyone I've ever met, or they're not being honest.

"Teamwork is a constant balancing act between self-interest and group interest."

SUSAN M. CAMPBELL

LIFE PROMISES

God blesses those who patiently endure testing and temptation. Afterward they will receive the crown of life that God has promised to those who love him.

JAMES 1:12

Since God in his mercy has given us this new way, we never give up.

2 CORINTHIANS 4:1

With God's help we will do mighty things.

PSALM 60:12

You Win Some . . .

It's important to remember that every Saturday, half the teams playing college football lose their games. It's just a fact of life. Our game against Texas in 2005 was a marquee matchup—the second game of the year, number two against number four, and the first time the two schools had ever played each other. With all the buildup and the national television audience, it was a game that everyone wanted to see. And we lost. So what did we do? Did we pack up and say, "No way we're going to win the national championship this year. We might as well focus on 2006"? The question wasn't whether we had won or lost; the question was, how should we respond to that outcome? We still had nine games to go. That's the way it is in life. You're going to have some major disappointments. And you're going to enjoy some success. You have to face both with equal tenacity, with equal heart.

"It's a rough road that leads to heights of greatness."

SENECA

LIFE PROMISES

Study this Book of Instruction continually. Meditate on it day and night so you will be sure to obey everything written in it. Only then will you prosper and succeed in all you do.

JOSHUA 1:8

If you are faithful in little things, you will be faithful in large ones. But if you are dishonest in little things, you won't be honest with greater responsibilities.

LUKE 16:10

Anyone who belongs to Christ has become a new person. The old life is gone; a new life has begun!

2 CORINTHIANS 5:17

Learn from Your Mistakes

When something goes wrong, our tendency is to just kick ourselves. But if we do that, we don't learn from the mistake; we don't use the adversity for ultimate good. To avoid making that mistake, we came up with a three-step process that ensures we will respond in a positive way to adversity on the field:

1. Learn from it.
2. Learn specifically what the right way is.
3. Practice visualizing the right way until your consciousness accepts a picture of yourself performing correctly.

If you're having a problem in the workplace, if you're having a relationship difficulty with your spouse, if you're off track spiritually, discover what you're doing wrong, learn the right way, and then practice doing it over and over. Performing it correctly with practice is the key to making it part of your daily life.

LIFE PROMISES

Two people are better off than one,
for they can help each other succeed.
. . . Three are even better, for a triple-
braided cord is not easily broken.

ECCLESIASTES 4:9, 12

All of you should be of one mind.
Sympathize with each other. Love
each other as brothers and sisters.
Be tenderhearted, and keep a
humble attitude.

1 PETER 3:8

Don't be selfish; don't try to impress
others. Be humble, thinking of others
as better than yourselves. Don't look
out only for your own interests, but
take an interest in others, too.

PHILIPPIANS 2:3-4

THERE'S NO *I* IN TEAM

As human beings, we were not made only to achieve things. From the moment we're born to the moment we die, life is about relationships. True winners in the game of life will not look merely at goals and achievements. True winners who are part of a winning team will care more about the people beside them in the trenches than they will about the trophy at the end of the journey.

"Coming together is a beginning; keeping together is a process; working together is success."

HENRY FORD

LIFE PROMISES

Encourage each other and build each other up.

1 THESSALONIANS 5:11

You are the salt of the earth. . . . You are the light of the world—like a city on a hilltop that cannot be hidden. No one lights a lamp and then puts it under a basket. Instead, a lamp is placed on a stand, where it gives light to everyone in the house. In the same way, let your good deeds shine out for all to see, so that everyone will praise your heavenly Father.

MATTHEW 5:13-16

Think of ways to motivate one another to acts of love and good works.

HEBREWS 10:24

THE RIPPLE EFFECT

E very great team I've ever been a part of realizes that our winning or losing affects more than just the team. In 1991, our Youngstown State team won the national championship in Division I-AA. When we arrived home after the game, ten thousand screaming fans met us at the Youngstown airport. As we tried to make our way through the throng to the bus that would take us back to campus, an older gentleman pushed his way through the crowd to get to me. I could see in his eyes the hardness of the years that had passed. With tears streaming down his face, he said, "This is the greatest day in my life since V-E Day." This man had probably lived in Youngstown his whole life. After World War II, he'd probably worked in the mill, probably lost his job when the economy turned, and no doubt his family had struggled. It appeared that between the time of the Allies' victory in Europe and our team's victory on the football field, things hadn't gone very well for this man. But to know that our team had brought such joy to his heart, and to all of Youngstown, was a huge bonus. *Any* endeavor is a group journey. When you play for more than just yourself, you can achieve the inner satisfaction and peace of mind that come from being a part of something much larger than yourself.

LIFE PROMISES

Don't be selfish; don't try to impress
others. Be humble, thinking of others
as better than yourselves. Don't look
out only for your own interests, but
take an interest in others, too.

PHILIPPIANS 2:3-4

If any of you wants to be my follower,
you must turn from your selfish ways,
take up your cross daily, and follow me.
If you try to hang on to your life, you
will lose it. But if you give up your life
for my sake, you will save it.

LUKE 9:23-24

Majority Rule

Relationship coach Susan M. Campbell has said, "Teamwork is a constant balancing act between self-interest and group interest." We all have self-interest, and there will always be some players who have a hard time buying into the team concept—they're in it for themselves. If the majority of players care about the team, they can model that for the ones who don't quite get it. But if the majority are continuously self-obsessed, we will wind up with nothing but chaos.

"Try to forget yourself in the service of others.
For when we think too much of ourselves and our
own interests, we easily become despondent.
But when we work for others,
our efforts return to bless us."

SIDNEY POWELL

LIFE PROMISES

Two people are better off than one, for they can help each other succeed. . . . Three are even better, for a triple-braided cord is not easily broken.

ECCLESIASTES 4:9, 12

Encourage those who are timid. Take tender care of those who are weak. Be patient with everyone.

1 THESSALONIANS 5:14

Feed the hungry, and help those in trouble. Then your light will shine out from the darkness, and the darkness around you will be as bright as noon.

ISAIAH 58:10

A Team of Geese

When geese fly in formation, they travel about 70 percent faster than when they fly alone. Geese share leadership. When the lead goose tires, he or she rotates back into the "V," and another goose flies forward to become the leader. Geese keep company with the fallen. When a sick or weak goose drops out of the flight formation, at least one other goose will leave the formation to help and protect the weaker goose. By being part of a team, we, too, can accomplish much more, much faster. Words of encouragement and support (honking from behind) inspire and energize those on the front lines and help them to keep pace in spite of day-to-day pressures and fatigue. Finally, show compassion and active caring for your fellow man—a member of the ultimate team: humankind! The next time you see a formation of geese, remember that it is a reward, a challenge, and a privilege to be a contributing member of a team.

LIFE PROMISES

Faith is the confidence that what we hope for will actually happen; it gives us assurance about things we cannot see.

HEBREWS 11:1

Anything is possible if a person believes.

MARK 9:23

Blessed are those who believe without seeing me.

JOHN 20:29

OLD WARWICK

A man became lost while driving through the country. As he tried to read a map, he accidentally drove off the road into a ditch. Though he wasn't injured, his car was stuck deep in the mud. Seeing a farmhouse just down the road, the man walked over to ask for help. "Warwick can get you out of the ditch," the farmer said, pointing to an old mule standing in a field. The man looked at the haggard mule, and then looked back at the farmer, who just stood there, nodding. "Yep, old Warwick can do the job."

The man figured he had nothing to lose, so the two men and Warwick made their way back to the ditch.

After the farmer hitched the old mule to the car, he snapped the reins and shouted, "Pull, Fred! Pull, Jack! Pull, Ted! Pull, Warwick!" With very little effort, the lone mule pulled the car from the ditch.

The man was amazed. He thanked the farmer, patted the mule, and asked, "Why did you call out all those other names before you called Warwick?" The farmer grinned and said, "Old Warwick is just about blind. As long as he believes he's part of a team, he doesn't mind pulling."

JAMES W. MOORE

LIFE PROMISES

He will order his angels to protect you wherever you go.

PSALM 91:11

God has given each of you a gift from his great variety of spiritual gifts. Use them well to serve one another. Do you have the gift of speaking? Then speak as though God himself were speaking through you. Do you have the gift of helping others? Do it with all the strength and energy that God supplies. Then everything you do will bring glory to God through Jesus Christ.

1 PETER 4:10-11

When you pray, I will listen. If you look for me wholeheartedly, you will find me.

JEREMIAH 29:12-13

Follow My Voice

In the smoke and confusion that followed the 9/11 attack on the Pentagon, dazed employees looked for any way out. For many, all they heard was a booming voice, calling, "Listen to me. Listen to me. Follow my voice." That voice belonged to Army Lt. Col. Victor Correa, who disappeared into a wall of smoke to look for his colleagues. "Yours was the voice I heard," several people told him afterward. "All of us had a different function," Correa said, "and I knew what mine was."

RON KAMPEAS

"Whatever you do, don't do it halfway."

BOB BEAMON

LIFE PROMISES

Work with enthusiasm, as though you were working for the Lord rather than for people. Remember that the Lord will reward each one of us for the good we do.

EPHESIANS 6:7-8

Always work enthusiastically for the Lord, for you know that nothing you do for the Lord is ever useless.

1 CORINTHIANS 15:58

Whatever you do, do well.

ECCLESIASTES 9:10

WORK

Work is the foundation of all business, the source of all prosperity, and the parent of genius.

Work can do more to advance a youth than his own parents, be they ever so wealthy.

It is represented in the humblest savings and has laid the foundation of every fortune.

It is the salt that gives life its savor, but it must be loved before it can bestow its greatest blessing and achieve its greatest ends.

When loved, work makes life sweet, purposeful, and fruitful.

AUTHOR UNKNOWN

"Work is love made visible."

KHALIL GIBRAN

LIFE PROMISES

Good planning and hard work lead to prosperity, but hasty shortcuts lead to poverty.

PROVERBS 21:5

Patient endurance is what you need now, so that you will continue to do God's will. Then you will receive all that he has promised.

HEBREWS 10:36

Work brings profit, but mere talk leads to poverty!

PROVERBS 14:23

WALKING THE TALK

No matter what endeavor you pursue in life, if you want to succeed, you're going to have to work at it. As kids, we thought football was pure fun. We'd get a group of our buddies together and find a field to play. Those were fun days. But at some point, if playing football is what you choose to do with your life, there's going to be an element of hardship and toil. Likewise, a musician who chooses to master the piano will tell you that she loves music. But to truly do justice to the instrument, a pianist must practice hours every day, even after she becomes accomplished. Someone who wants to become a writer must take the time to study and learn more about the craft. Many people say, "I know I have a book in me," but until they sit down and put words on the page, it's just talk. Michael Jordan once said, "Coaches or players can say anything they want, but if they don't back it up with performance and hard work, the talking doesn't mean a thing." That's how success is achieved. You work at it bit by bit, day by day, one step here, another there. You fall, you get up, and you keep going.

LIFE PROMISES

Make it your goal to live a quiet life,
minding your own business and
working with your hands. . . . Then
people who are not Christians will
respect the way you live, and you
will not need to depend on others.

1 THESSALONIANS 4:11-12

To enjoy your work and accept your lot
in life—this is indeed a gift from God.

ECCLESIASTES 5:19

Pay careful attention to your own work,
for then you will get the satisfaction of
a job well done, and you won't need to
compare yourself to anyone else. For
we are each responsible for our own
conduct.

GALATIANS 6:4-5

BE WHO YOU ARE, NOT WHAT YOU DO

It's important to understand that work is not who you are; it's what you do. Many people get that backward and think their lives are defined by what they accomplish or by what positions they hold. My grandfather was a dairy farmer, and he never took a day off. Those cows had to get rid of their milk every day. My grandfather not only worked hard, but he was also the most spiritual man I have ever known. He died at age eighty-seven, sitting in his rocking chair, his Bible in his lap, opened to Psalm 23. He had a heart issue and a bit of cancer, but he was still farming into his eighties. He loved that he was providing people with something important, something sustaining, and he farmed with a passion. Given how much time my grandfather invested in his dairy farm, it would have been easy for him to define himself by his profession. All he did was work. Nevertheless, he was one of the most well-rounded people I've ever known. He gave to people. He cared. He made time for his family. Dairy farming was what he *did*. But it didn't define who he *was*.

LIFE PROMISES

Wealth from get-rich-quick schemes quickly disappears; wealth from hard work grows over time.

PROVERBS 13:11

Remember this—a farmer who plants only a few seeds will get a small crop. But the one who plants generously will get a generous crop.

2 CORINTHIANS 9:6

Be strong and courageous, for your work will be rewarded.

2 CHRONICLES 15:7

COLIN POWELL ON WORK

Whenever you start—give it your best. The opportunities are there to be anything you want to be. But wanting to be someone isn't enough; dreaming about it isn't enough; thinking about it isn't enough. You've got to study for it, work for it, fight for it with all your heart and soul, because nobody is going to hand it to you.

GENERAL COLIN POWELL

"Coaches and players can say anything they want, but if they don't back it up with performance and hard work, the talking doesn't mean a thing."

MICHAEL JORDAN

LIFE PROMISES

Always work enthusiastically for the Lord, for you know that nothing you do for the Lord is ever useless.

1 CORINTHIANS 15:58

Train yourself to be godly. Physical training is good, but training for godliness is much better, promising benefits in this life and in the life to come.

1 TIMOTHY 4:7-8

Let us run with endurance the race God has set before us.

HEBREWS 12:1

No Pain, No Gain

The truth is, work is really a gift from God. In the beginning, God gave people meaningful work to do. It's part of the fabric of our lives. And I've always believed that anything good in life takes effort. If you want to keep your body healthy, it takes work. If you want to advance in your career, you have to work at it. Your conscious desire to care and give to others takes work. Your spiritual life takes work. Your family life takes work. It's important to get work in its proper perspective, to see it for the gift it is.

"Even if you're on the right track,
you'll get run over if you just sit there."

WILL ROGERS

PART THREE
THE EPITOME OF
SUCCESS

"Do not settle for anything less than an extraordinary life."

AUTHOR UNKNOWN

LIFE PROMISES

Don't be afraid, for I am with you. Don't be discouraged, for I am your God. I will strengthen you and help you. I will hold you up with my victorious right hand.

ISAIAH 41:10

Fix your thoughts on what is true, and honorable, and right, and pure, and lovely, and admirable. Think about things that are excellent and worthy of praise.

PHILIPPIANS 4:8

Seek the Kingdom of God above all else, and live righteously, and he will give you everything you need.

MATTHEW 6:33

PROMISE YOURSELF . . .

to be so strong that nothing can disturb your peace
of mind

to look at the sunny side of everything and make
your optimism come true

to think only of the best

to be just as enthusiastic about the success of
others as you are about your own

to forget the mistakes of the past and press on to
the greater achievements of the future

to share the greater achievements of the future

to give so much time to the improvement of
yourself that you have no time to criticize
others

to be too large for worry, too strong for fear, and too
happy to permit the presence of trouble

LIFE PROMISES

You must clothe yourselves with tenderhearted mercy, kindness, humility, gentleness, and patience. Make allowances for each other's faults, and forgive anyone who offends you.

COLOSSIANS 3:12-13

When you obey my commandments, you remain in my love, just as I obey my Father's commandments and remain in his love.

JOHN 15:10

The LORD will withhold no good thing from those who do what is right.

PSALM 84:11

Colin Powell's Rules

1. It ain't as bad as you think. It will look better in the morning.
2. Get mad, then get over it.
3. Avoid having your ego so close to your position that when your position falls, your ego goes with it.
4. It can be done!
5. Be careful what you choose. You may get it.
6. Don't let adverse facts stand in the way of a good decision.
7. You can't make someone else's choices. You shouldn't let someone else make yours.
8. Check small things.
9. Share credit.
10. Remain calm. Be kind.
11. Have a vision. Be demanding.
12. Don't take the counsel of your fears or naysayers.
13. Perpetual optimism is a force multiplier.

"Start by doing what's necessary, then what's possible, and suddenly you are doing the impossible."

ST. FRANCIS OF ASSISI

LIFE PROMISES

God blesses those who are humble, for they will inherit the whole earth. God blesses those who hunger and thirst for justice, for they will be satisfied. God blesses those who are merciful, for they will be shown mercy. God blesses those whose hearts are pure, for they will see God. God blesses those who work for peace, for they will be called the children of God. God blesses those who are persecuted for doing right, for the Kingdom of Heaven is theirs.

MATTHEW 5:5-10

Work hard to prove that you really are among those God has called and chosen. Do these things, and you will never fall away. Then God will give you a grand entrance into the eternal Kingdom of our Lord and Savior Jesus Christ.

2 PETER 1:10-11

You Are at the Top When . . .

1. You have made friends with your past, and you are focused on the present and optimistic about your future.
2. You have the love of friends and the respect of your enemies.
3. You are filled with faith, hope, and love, and you live without anger, greed, guilt, envy, or thoughts of revenge.
4. You love the unlovable, give hope to the hopeless, friendship to the friendless, and encouragement to the discouraged.
5. You can look back in forgiveness, forward in hope, down in compassion, and up with gratitude.
6. You are secure in who (and whose) you are, so you are at peace with God and in fellowship with humanity.
7. You recognize, confess, develop, and use your God-given physical, mental, and spiritual abilities to the glory of God and for the benefit of humankind.
8. You stand in front of the Creator of the universe, and he says to you, "Well done, my good and faithful servant."

LIFE PROMISES

He renews my strength. He guides me along right paths, bringing honor to his name.

PSALM 23:3

If we are faithful to the end, trusting God just as firmly as when we first believed, we will share in all that belongs to Christ.

HEBREWS 3:14

This is the secret: Christ lives in you. This gives you assurance of sharing his glory.

COLOSSIANS 1:27

Dream Big

If there were ever a time to dare, to make a difference,
to embark on something worth doing, it is now.
Not for any grand cause, necessarily—
but for something that tugs at your heart,
something that's your aspiration,
something that's your dream.

You owe it to yourself to make your days here count.
Have fun.
Dig deep.
Stretch.

Dream big. . . .

Believe in the incredible power of the human mind.
Of doing something that makes a difference.
Of working hard.
Of laughing and hoping.
Of lazy afternoons.
Of lasting friends.
Of all the things that will cross your path this year.
The start of something new brings the hope of
        something great.
Anything is possible.
There is only one you.
And you will pass this way only once.
Do it right.

AUTHOR UNKNOWN

LIFE PROMISES

Well done, my good and faithful servant.

MATTHEW 25:21

No eye has seen, no ear has heard, and no mind has imagined what God has prepared for those who love him.

1 CORINTHIANS 2:9

It is no longer I who live, but Christ lives in me.

GALATIANS 2:20

I press on to possess that perfection for which Christ Jesus first possessed me. . . . I have not achieved it, but I focus on this one thing: Forgetting the past and looking forward to what lies ahead, I press on to reach the end of the race and receive the heavenly prize for which God, through Christ Jesus, is calling us.

PHILIPPIANS 3:12-14

God's Hall of Fame

The Hall of Fame is only good as long as time
  shall be,
But keep in mind, God's Hall of Fame is for eternity!
To have your name inscribed up there is greater
  more by far,
Than all the praise and all the fame of any man-
  made star!

AUTHOR UNKNOWN

"Fame is vapor,
Popularity an accident,
And riches take wings.
Only one thing endures—character."

HORACE GREELEY

CREDITS

"The Guy in the Glass" is copyright ©1934 by Dale Wimbrow. All rights reserved. Used by permission.

"Coach Wooden on Criticism and Praise" is adapted from *Wooden: A Lifetime of Observations and Reflections On and Off the Court* by John Wooden and Steve Jamison (Chicago: Contemporary Books, 1997), 146–147.

"A Simple Gesture" by John W. Schlatter is taken from *Condensed Chicken Soup for the Soul* by Jack Canfield, Mark Victor Hansen, and Patty Hansen (Deerfield Beach, FL: Health Communications, 1996), 10–11.

"Giving When It Counts" is taken from "On Courage" by Dan Millman, in *Chicken Soup for the Soul* by Jack Canfield and Mark Victor Hansen (Deerfield Beach, FL: Health Communications, 1993), 26–27.

"Old Warwick" is adapted from *Some Folks Feel the Rain: Others Just Get Wet* by James W. Moore (Nashville: Dimensions for Living, 1999), 104–105.

"Follow My Voice" is taken from "Discipline, training saved lives in aftermath of Pentagon attack," by Ron Kampeas, Associated Press, September 17, 2001. Article can be read online at http://www.cjonline.com/stories/091701/ter_training.shtml.

SCRIPTURE INDEX

ABOUT THE AUTHOR

JIM TRESSEL is the head coach of the Ohio State Buckeyes football team. Since taking over the reins in 2001, he has guided the Buckeyes to nine bowl appearances, including seven BCS games; seven ten-win seasons; six Big Ten titles; and the 2002 national championship. Prior to coming to Ohio State, Tressel spent fifteen seasons as the head coach at Youngstown State University, where he was selected four times as the Division I-AA National Coach of the Year. Entering the 2010 season, Coach Tressel has an overall coaching record of 229-78-2 and is ranked twelfth all-time in Division I coaching victories.

In the course of his coaching career, Tressel has been named the Chevrolet National Coach of the Year ('93, '94, and '97); the American Coaches Association National Coach of the Year ('91, '94, and '02); the Eddie Robinson National Coach of the Year ('94 and '02); and the AFCA Regional Coach of the Year ('87 and '93). He has also been selected seven times as Ohio Coach of the Year.

Coach Tressel is actively involved with the American Football Coaches Association, the Fellowship of Christian Athletes, Alpha Tau Omega, The Ohio State University Medical Center, and the William Oxley Thompson Memorial Library.

He and his wife also work on behalf of the Alzheimer's Association of Central Ohio, the Columbus Children's Hospital, the Tressel Family Fund for Cancer Prevention Research, Ronald McDonald House, the Youngstown State University Minority Student Endowment, the Mount Carmel School of Nursing, and the Jim and Ellen Tressel Athletic Scholarship Fund.

Coach Tressel and his wife, Ellen, live in Upper Arlington, Ohio. They are the parents of four children: Zak, Carlee, Eric, and Whitney.

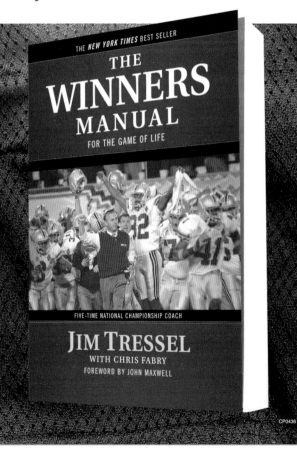